Masonic Enlightenment

Edited by Michael R. Poll

Masonic Enlightenment

A Cornerstone Book
Published by Cornerstone Book Publishers
Copyright © 2006 by Michael R. Poll

Published by Cornerstone Book Publishers
Lafayette, LA
USA

First Cornerstone Edition - 2006

www.cornerstonepublishers.com

ISBN: 1-887560-75-0

MADE IN THE USA

Table of Contents

THE LANDMARKS OF MASONRY
by Silas H. Shepherd 1

THE WEBB RITUAL IN THE UNITED STATES
by Silas H. Shepherd 10

THE MEANING OF INITIATION
by Frank C. Higgins 18

THE DOCTRINE OF THE BALANCE
by Joseph Fort Newton 22

OPERATIVE MASONRY: EARLY DAYS IN THE MASONIC ERA
by Robert I. Clegg 27

MASONIC JURISPRUDENCE
by Roscoe Pound 36

FREEMASONS IN THE AMERICAN REVOLUTION
by Charles S. Lobingier 48

A BIRD'S-EYE VIEW OF MASONIC HISTORY
by H.L. Haywood 58

WOMAN AND FREEMASONRY
by Dudley Wright 71

IN THE INTERESTS OF THE BRETHREN
by Rudyard Kipling 93

THE EGYPTIAN INFLUENCE ON OUR MASONIC CEREMONIAL AND
RITUAL
by Thomas Ross 105

ANDERSON'S CONSTITUTIONS OF 1723
by Lionel Vibert 114

THE RISE AND DEVELOPMENT OF ANTI-MASONRY IN AMERICA,
1737-1826
by J. Hugo Tatsch 126

THE SPIRITUAL SIGNIFICANCE OF FREEMASONRY
by Silas H. Shepherd 139

ROSICRUCIANISM IN FREEMASONRY
by H.V.B. Voorhis 143

THE NEW ATLANTIS AND FREEMASONRY
by A. J. B. Milborne 151

THE FORTY-SEVENTH PROBLEM OF EUCLID
by C.C. Hunt 155

MASONRY AND WORLD PEACE
by Joseph Fort Newton 160

Masonic Enlightenment

THE LANDMARKS OF MASONRY
by Silas H. Shepherd

Editor's Note: This paper was written in 1915 and should not be considered the current opinion of Grand Lodges in the United States. The text of the paper is, however, very useful in understanding how the Grand Lodges in the U.S. view the concept of Landmarks in general.

The "Ancient Landmarks" and "Landmarks of Masonry" are terms which appear throughout the literature of Masonry, and are the source of deep study by many Craftsmen who have devoted time, talent and genius to promote the best interests of our fraternity.

On the subject of "landmarks," as on the subjects of history and symbolism, there is a great diversity of opinion, both by Grand Lodges and by individuals, and the need of a comparison of ideas which are held by those who have made the subject a study was the cause which prompted us to compile this article.

"What is a landmark?" is a debatable question. It has been answered in part by definitions; it has also been answered by enumerating certain laws or customs which are considered landmarks by the authors of the compilations; it has also been considered a proper subject for legislation by some Grand Lodges and they have enacted laws as to what are to be considered landmarks in their jurisdiction.

After the organization of the Premier Grand Lodge in 1717, the "Charges of a Freemason" were extracted from the old manuscript copies and a set of thirty-nine "General Regulations" were adopted, the last of which reads in part as follows: "Every Annual Grand Lodge has an inherent power and authority to make new Regulations, or to alter these, for the real benefit of this ancient Fraternity: Provided, always, that the old Land-Marks be carefully preserved." This is the earliest mention of landmarks in connection with Freemasonry.

Neither at that time nor at any subsequent period can we find any enumeration of landmarks by the Grand Lodge of England, "Ancient," "Modern" or United.

On Oct. 19th, 1810, the Lodge of Promulgation resolved "that it appears to this Lodge, that the ceremony of Installation of Masters of Lodges, is one of the two Land Marks of the Craft and ought to be observed.

We are left entirely in the dark as to what they considered the other landmark. This is the only case where we have been able to find any attempt to say how many or what constituted a landmark until 1856 when the Grand

Lodge of Minnesota adopted a list of twenty-six articles which had the force of landmarks, which was two years earlier than Bro. Albert Mackey enumerated his list which has been generally considered the first attempt to enumerate them.

We will give the definition of landmarks by several learned brethren.

"Of the nature of the Landmarks of Masonry, there has been some diversity of opinion among writers; but perhaps the safest method is to restrict them to those ancient, and therefore universal, customs of the Order, which either gradually grew into operation as rules of action, or if at once enacted by any competent authority, were enacted at a period so remote, that no account of their origin is to be found in the records of history." (Albert G. Mackey, *Mas. Jur.* page 15.)

"The very definition of Landmarks shows that an enumeration of them is scarcely possible. All we can know is that it is a law or a custom that has existed from time immemorial. If any universal usage exists, and has existed so long that its origin is unknown, it is a Landmark." (Josiah Drummond, *Maine Masonic Text Book.*)

"With respect to the Landmarks of Masonry, some restrict them to the O.B., signs, tokens and words. Others include the ceremony of initiation, passing and raising; and the form, dimensions and supports; the ground, situation and covering; the ornaments, furniture and jewels of a Lodge, or their characteristic symbols. Some think that the order has no landmarks beyond its peculiar secrets. (Geo. Oliver, *Dict. Symb. Mas.*)

"We assume those principles of action to be Landmarks which have existed from time immemorial, whether in the written or unwritten law; which are identified with the form and essence of the society; which, the great majority agree, cannot be changed, and which every Mason is bound to maintain intact, under the most solemn and inviolable sanctions." (Simons, *Prin. of Mas. Juris.*)

"Those fixed tenets by which the limits of Freemasonry may be known and preserved." (*Dictionary of Freemasonry*, Morris.)

"The Landmarks of Masonry are those ancient principles and practices which mark out and distinguish Freemasonry as such, and they are the source of Masonic Jurisprudence." (Lockwood's *Mas. Law and Practice*, Page 14.)

"My idea of an Ancient Landmark is a rule or usage of the Premier Grand Lodge which can not be abrogated, without cutting off the offending

Body from the Universal Craft." (W. J. Hughan.)

"A belief in God, our Father; in the immortality of the soul; in the brotherhood of man; and in the necessary practice of all the moral and social virtue, were the essentials, our duty to God, our country, our neighbor and ourselves, was everywhere and universally inculcated. These we take to be the Landmarks of the Order." (John Q. A. Fellows, *Proc. G. L. of La.*, 1889.)

"A 'Landmark' that cannot be established by the writings of the fathers, or other recognized authorities, to have been the rule or belief among Freemasons in 1723 and before, or that is not now generally accepted as such, can hardly be held as Landmark. (H. B. Grant, *Const. G. L. of Ky.*, 1910.)

"A Landmark, to be a Landmark, must command the universal respect and observance of all Masons." (T. S. Parvin, *Iowa Proc. 1889*, Page 106, cor. report.)

"The fundamental principles of the Ancient Operative Masonry were few and simple, and they were not called landmarks. Each lodge was independent of every other, and there was no superior authority over all. Each was composed of Apprentices and FellowCrafts. Each had its Master and Wardens, and these were elected by vote of all the members. The ancient charges show by what principles the relations of those of the fellowship to each other were regulated; and these may not improperly be said to have been the 'landmarks' of the Craft." (Albert Pike, *Iowa Proc. 1888*, Page 156, cor. report.)

"The Old Landmarks were, in fact, the secrets which existed amongst the Operative Masons in the days when they alone supplied the membership of the Craft." (W. B. Hextall, *Ars. Q. C. XXV*, Page 91.)

"The Ancient Landmarks of Freemasonry, like all other landmarks material or symbolical, can only preserve their stability, when they reach down to sure foundations. When the philosophic student unearths the underlying rock on which our Ancient Landmarks rest, he finds our sure foundations in the triple dogma Georgia — of the Fatherhood of God, the Brotherhood of Man, and the Life to come. All laws, customs and methods that obtain amongst us and do not ultimately find footholds

on this basis, are thereby earmarked as conventions and conveniences, no way partaking of the nature of Ancient Landmarks." (Chetwode Crawley, *Ars. Q. C. XXIII.*)

The Masonic Congress at Chicago in 1893 defined the landmarks thus:

"The Ancient Landmarks are those fundamental principles which characterize Masonry as defined by the Charges of a Freemason, and without which the institution cannot be identified as Masonry, combined with the essentials of the unwritten language by which brethren distinguished each other as Masons."

Having given a few of the definitions of landmarks by individual brethren and the collective opinion of the Masonic Congress at Chicago, 1893, which was very representative of Masonic scholarship in America, we will give what each Grand Lodge in the United States does or does not do in respect to landmarks.

Alabama— Alabama recognizes as the landmarks the Old Charges of 1722 by Anderson.

Arizona— Arizona is the only Grand Lodge on which we have no authentic information. We have searched the proceedings in vain to find what they hold to be the landmarks and have not been favored with a reply to our letter of inquiry.

Arkansas— Arkansas has no enumeration of the landmarks.

California— California has no legislation on the subject of landmarks, but as a general proposition accepts Mackey's twenty-five.

Colorado— Colorado has never adopted a particular list of landmarks, having been governed by the old constitutions and those published in Mackey's Encyclopedia.

Connecticut— Connecticut has adopted as its code the treatise known as "Lockwood's Masonic Law and Practice" and by inference holds to the specification of Landmarks contained therein.

Delaware— No mention is made of Landmarks in the Constitution of 1909 and no list of landmarks appears in their code.

District of Columbia— The District of Columbia accepts as the landmarks the twenty-five laid down by Mackey.

Florida— Florida has never taken any action on the subject of landmarks.

Georgia— Georgia has no list of landmarks. Art. IV of the Constitution of 1909 reads: "The Grand Lodge shall have power as follows: To propose, enact and establish new regulations for the government of the Craft within its jurisdiction, and the same to alter, amend, explain or repeal, not contravening the ancient landmarks of the Order." Edict 177 reads: "The Unwritten Law, the Immemorial Usages, the Landmarks and the like, of Masonry, are not repealed by the adoption of any Constitution and By-Laws, nor is it in the power of any man or body of men to change, alter or repeal these or any of them."

Idaho— Idaho has no legislation defining or enumerating what landmarks are.

Illinois— Illinois has no legislation defining landmarks. Illinois follows Robbins and Drummond on this subject.

Indiana— No mention is made in the Indiana Constitution of Landmarks; and no list of landmarks appears in their code.

Iowa— Iowa has no list of landmarks. The following is Sec. 5, Gen. Law: "The unwritten laws of this jurisdiction consist of the time honored customs and usages of the Ancient Free and Accepted Masons, of general recognition, as they are found in the traditional and historic records of Freemasonry and adapted to the conditions and time in which we live, together with such rules for application as will perpetuate its integrity and usefulness, and not repugnant to its written laws."

Kansas— Kansas does not consider the landmarks a subject for legislation. With their code they publish the "Bassett notes" containing list of landmarks by Mackey, Morris, Simons and Lockwood for the information of the brethren.

Kentucky— The declaration at the beginning of the Constitution of the Grand Lodge of Kentucky 1908, reads: "The Grand Lodge of Kentucky acknowledges belief in God to be the great fundamental principle and Landmark of Masonry upon which our fraternity is erected." The Ancient Charges of 1723 are printed on pages 200-205, and on pages 209 to 240 are the "Ancient Landmarks with supporting evidence," by H. B. Grant, 54 in number. (G. W. Speth reviewed them in *Ars. Q. C. VII.*)

Louisiana— Louisiana Constitution of 1902, Sec. 4, second paragraph, considering the powers of the Grand Lodge reads: "It may make all laws and regulations necessary for the government of the lodges and brethren under its jurisdiction, and for the propagation and advancement of the true principles and work of Ancient Freemasonry, not inconsistent with the provisions of this Constitution, the old Charges of Free and Accepted Masons of 1723 hereunto annexed, or the ancient usages and landmarks of the Order." Edict 44 reads: "That the only written landmarks are those in the ancient Charges of the Craft, forming part of the Constitution of the Grand Lodge; and the unwritten, those contained in the ceremonies of initiation, and the ties which bind us together as Masons: Nor is it proper by legislation to make any new obligations with penalties attached, nor for a lodge to attempt, by resolution, to define the landmarks of the Craft."

Maine— Maine has no legislation as to what landmarks are. They follow Josiah Drummond's ideas.

Maryland— Maryland has no list of landmarks. Art. II Constitution of 1906 defines the duty of the Grand Lodge; among other duties is one "to preserve and maintain the Ancient Landmarks." Article XXIX reads: "In all cases not particularly provided for in this Constitution, the Grand Lodge shall adhere to, and be governed by the Ancient Rules and Regulations of Masonry."

Massachusetts— Massachusetts has never adopted any list of landmarks. They "feel safer in cultivating a spirit of reverence for the ancient customs and practices of the Order" than in attempting to define the Landmarks.

Michigan— Michigan has no list of landmarks. The following is taken from the preface of the Michigan Blue Book of 1911: "The first place in the volume— the place of honor—has been assigned to the "Ancient Charges and Regulations" not because they are, in form, binding on us, but because they are universally recognized as the beginning and basis of all the "written law" of the Craft; and also because they embody many of those "Ancient Landmarks" which give "metes and bounds" to the Rules and Regulations of Symbolic Masonry."

Minnesota— Minnesota has adopted Mackey's twenty-five landmarks.

Mississippi— The Old Charges and Regulations of 1723 are printed as a part of the Constitution of 1903. Frederic Speed enumerates eight landmarks which are sub-divided into many sections and were found among the papers of the late P. G. M. Giles M. Hillyer.

Missouri— Missouri has no list of landmarks. Bro. John D. Vincil, conceded to be one of the best posted men on jurisprudence, disclaimed knowing what the landmarks were.

Montana— Montana has the customary exception to its powers, viz: "Provided, always, that the ancient landmarks of the order will be held inviolate." Montana has no list of landmarks.

Nebraska— Nebraska has never decided on any particular list of landmarks.

Nevada— Nevada has a list of 39 landmarks which were adopted in 1872.

New Hampshire— New Hampshire never officially defined what the landmarks are.

New Jersey— New Jersey has a list of 10 landmarks which were adopted in 1903. New Jersey Proceedings of 1903 contains an interesting report on these 10 landmarks by the Committee on Jurisprudence.

New Mexico— New Mexico has adopted Mackey's 25 landmarks.

New York— "The Ancient Landmarks are those principles of Masonic belief, government, and polity which are the only part of Masonic Law or rule that may never be altered or disturbed, and such of them as are lawful to be written are usually, but not wholly, engrafted in a written Constitution." (*Const. G. L. of N. Y.* 1913.) On page 63 and 64 of the same book are the landmarks as defined by P. G. M. Joseph D. Evans, 10 in number.

North Carolina— North Carolina has no list of landmarks, nor legislation defining them.

North Dakota— North Dakota has no legislation defining or enumerating landmarks. They include in their Constitution the Ancient Charges and Regulations.

Ohio— The Ohio Code states that "the Old Charges contain the fundamental laws" which is practically giving them sanction as landmarks. The Old Charges are a part of the Code.

Oklahoma— At the Feb. 1915 Communication of the Grand Lodge of Oklahoma, they acknowledged and practically adopted the 25 landmarks of Mackey.

Oregon— Oregon has adopted Mackey's 25 landmarks.

Pennsylvania— The Ahiman Rezon contains the following on landmarks: "The Grand Lodge is the supreme Masonic authority except that it cannot change, alter or destroy the Ancient Landmarks." "The Past Grand Masters shall be regarded as the conservators of the ancient usages, customs and Landmarks." No landmarks are enumerated.

Rhode Island and Providence Plantations— Rhode Island has no list of landmarks. The following is from the preamble to the Constitution of 1897: "Every Grand Lodge has inherent power and authority to make local ordinances and new regulations, for its own benefit and the good of Masonry in general—provided, always, that the ancient landmarks be carefully preserved."

South Carolina— South Carolina has adopted Mackey's list of 25 landmarks.

South Dakota— South Dakota Constitution of 1912 states that the Landmarks as defined by Dr. Mackey have binding force on South Dakota Masons.

Tennessee— Tennessee has a list of 15 landmarks which are almost identical with those enumerated by Simons

Texas— Chapter 2, Article 1, Sec. 4, of the Texas Code reads: "The Book of Constitutions of Masonry originally prepared by Dr. Anderson, approved A.D. 1723, contains the system of ancient laws and customs of the Craft, and is recognized as binding on points where this Constitution is silent; the old charges therein shall be appended entire hereto." This is the only light we can obtain on what the Grand Lodge of Texas thinks the landmarks are.

Utah— Utah holds the "Old Charges of a Freemason" to be the landmarks. Christopher Diehl, a well known correspondence writer for years, had a list of landmarks which he submitted to the Grand Lodge of Utah; but they were never adopted.

Vermont— Vermont adheres to the list of 25 landmarks of Mackey.

Washington— Washington Constitution of 1913, Sec. 13, says: The action of Freemasons in the Grand Lodge and in their Lodges, and in their individual capacity is regulated and controlled 1. By Ancient Landmarks, and other unwritten laws of Masonry. 2. By Written- Constitutions, and general or special legislation. 3. By Usages, Customs and judicial action." "Sec. 14 Landmarks.— The Ancient Landmarks include those principles of Masonic government and polity which should never be altered or disturbed." No landmarks are enumerated.

West Virginia— West Virginia has a list of 7 landmarks, a report on landmarks for the information of the brethren is given first place in the West Virginia Masonic Text Book. It contains lists by Mackey, Simons, Morris and Pike.

Wyoming— Wyoming Grand Lodge considers the landmarks too deep a subject to comment on and does not attempt an enumeration of them.

Wisconsin— Wisconsin has no legislation defining or enumerating the landmarks, but gives Mackey's 25 in code for their information of the brethren.

To recapitulate we find District of Columbia, Minnesota, New Mexico, Oklahoma, Oregon, South Dakota, South Carolina, Vermont, Virginia adopt Mackey's list of 25. Alabama, Louisiana, Mississippi, Ohio, Texas, Utah hold the old charges to contain the landmarks. Those having list of landmarks of their own and the number are Connecticut, Kentucky, New Jersey, Nevada, Tennessee and West Virginia. The others all hold that the landmarks are the most important and fundamental law of Masonry, but do not consider a list made by any man or body of men sufficiently accurate to apply to them.

In concluding this compilation we can hardly refrain from expressing a thought or so which has forced itself upon us. The live questions of Masonic Jurisprudence are most all affected by the views entertained in regard to landmarks; take for example the question of physical qualification. To those who hold the view of Mackey, Lockwood, Simons and others that it is a landmark it appears quite different from the view taken by those who hold that the only landmarks are the fundamental principles of Fatherhood of God and Brotherhood of Man.

We can hardly grasp the logic of why the physical qualification should be deemed a landmark and leave to the local custom column the rule that an entered apprentice serve seven years before being passed. They were both the necessary rules of an operative Craft and the need of a longer apprenticeship would appear to be greater than the strict conformity.

Again the prerogatives of a Grand Master largely stand or fall on interpretation of the landmarks, as do also our recognition of other Grand Bodies.

We might make many comparisons and comments but believe that the landmarks, like the history and symbolism of Masonry, must be left mostly to individual interpretation. For those who wish to read on landmarks and have not already done so we would refer them to: Mackey's *"Masonic Jurisprudence."* Simon's *"Principles of Masonic Jurisprudence."* Lockwood's *"Masonic Law and Practice." Maine Masonic Text Book. Macoy-Oliver Encyclopedia. Kansas Code* 1913. Bassett notes. *Kentucky Book of Const.* 1910. Grant notes. *Iowa Proceedings* 1888-1889. *Ars. Q. C. Vol. VII, XXIV, XXV. Mississippi Const.* 1903. *New Jersey Proc.* 1903. *Code of Dist. of Col.* 1905, p. 191. The correspondence reports of Bro. Joseph Robbins of Ill., and Bro. Upton of Wash., are rich in comments.

THE WEBB RITUAL IN THE UNITED STATES
by Silas H. Shepherd

The year 1717 will ever stand out as a prominent date in the history of Freemasonry. Since then we have voluminous written and printed records; before then we had but about a hundred old manuscript charges, a few mentions of Freemasonry in biography and laws, and a very few lodge minutes.

Previous to 1717, the rituals, or forms and ceremonies of reception of candidates and other work of the lodge, were most probably given in the language and manner the presiding officer chose. It may have been in a "set form of words," which form was transmitted orally from one generation to another.

Soon after the "revival," or the organization of the Grand Lodge in 1717, Rev. James Anderson, the author of the "Book of Constitutions" of 1723, and Dr. John T. Desaguliers, the master mind of the organization, arranged the lectures into the form of questions and answers for the first time, and this was adopted by the Grand Lodge as the authentic lectures. (1)

In 1732, Martin Clare revised the lectures and made a few Christian applications which were not in strict conformity to the cosmopolitan character of the fraternity. Dr. Thos. Manningham and Thos. Dunkery were the next to "improve the work" and Dr. Manningham's prayer is still used, with slight modifications in opening a lodge and at the reception of candidates. Thos. Dunkerly is said to have given the theological ladder its three principal rounds. In 1763, Wm. Hutchinson again revised and "improved" the lectures and gave more Christian applications to their rites and ceremonies. (2)

The greatest of all ritualists, however, was William Preston who was made a Mason in a lodge of "Antients," in 1763, and soon after induced that lodge to be reconstituted by the "Moderns." In 1767 he became master of his lodge. He believed that Freemasonry should not only be a progressive moral science, but that it should have an educational value in giving its votaries more knowledge of the liberal arts and sciences. His "Illustrations of Masonry" was the result, and no book having more influence has ever been written on Masonry. He was the father of the monitor. By 1774 he had completed his system of "work" and established a school of instruction, and from that time to the present the Preston "work" has been, and undoubtedly far into the future it will continue to be, one of the most potent influences of the ritual. Preston's "work" continued to be the standard work for the Grand Lodge of England until 1813, when the "United Grand Lodge" adopted the Hemming lectures. The Hemming lectures differ in many particulars from the Preston. The Preston lectures are still given once a year in England under the auspices of a foundation made for that purpose.

When Freemasonry was first established in America is an open question. We are not quite sure that the stone with the date 1606 is really a Masonic stone of that date, or that Mordecai Campanell and his companions conferred the degrees of Masonry in 1656 at Newport, R. I. (3) Neither are we certain as to where Freemasonry was first practiced in this country by authority of the Grand Lodge of England after 1717. It is, however, well known that lodges were established in the colonies and that Daniel Coxe, Henry Price and James Graeme were issued deputations as Provincial Grand Masters.

The ritual of the English lodges would naturally have been the one used in the English colonies, and in this connection it is well to call attention to the fact that the "Grand Lodge of England according to the old Institutions," or "Ancients," was established in 1751, and from that time until 1813 chartered lodges in all the colonies. In many of the colonies there were two conflicting Provincial Grand Lodges.

In the establishment of the "Ancient" Grand Lodge changes were made which were of considerable importance. (4) Uniformity was not accomplished in England until 1813, and it has not yet been attained, and probably never will be attained, in America. Pennsylvania still retains the "Ancient work."

After the Colonies had declared their independence of Great Britain, the Provincial Grand Lodges naturally declared their independence of the Grand Lodges to which they owed their origin. Each was then a sovereign Grand Lodge.

To return to the lectures; they took the form of the place whence they came, and were quite probably not transmitted with a great degree of accuracy, and were not very uniform in the United States at the close of the Eighteenth century.

Thos. Smith Webb was born in Boston, Mass., October 13, 1771, and became a printer or book binder. Early in life he became a Mason and a teacher of Masonry. In 1797 he published the *"Freemason's Monitor."* He subsequently did more for Masonry than almost any one else in his day, and was probably personally instrumental in founding the "American Rite," or system of degrees of Royal Arch, Council and Commandery. What we are particularly interested in, however, is his connection with ancient craft Masonry.

About the close of the eighteenth century a printer named Hanmer came to America and brought the Preston work. He communicated it to Webb. Soon afterward Webb abridged it, arranged it differently, as to sections, and taught this revision to Benjamin Gleason, Henry Fowle, Bro. Snow, and others. In 1806 a joint committee of six, of which Bros. Gleason and

Fowle were members, met and agreed upon the Webb work as the standard work of Massachusetts and New Hampshire. Bro. Jeremy Cross claimed to have received his work from this committee. (5) In an address before the Grand Lodge of Vermont in 1859 G. M. Philip Tucker gave much valuable information from which we excerpt the following:

"About the year 1800 — twelve years after the publication of Preston's Illustrations an English brother, whose name I have been unable to obtain, came to Boston and taught the English Lectures as they had been arranged by Preston. The Grand Lodge of Massachusetts approved them and they were taught by Thomas S. Webb and Henry Fowle, of Boston, and Brother Snow, of Rhode Island. About the year 1801, Brother Benjamin Gleason, who was a student of Bro. Webb, received them from him, and embodied them in a private key of his own. About the year 1805, Bro. Gleason was employed by the Grand Lodge of Massachusetts to teach all the Subordinate Lodges of that jurisdiction, and was paid for that service, fifteen hundred dollars. To those lectures the Grand Lodge of Massachusetts still adheres, with a very slight variation in the Fellow Craft and Master's Degree. Bro. Snow afterwards changed and modified the Lectures he had received — mingling with them some changes from other sources — so that the system of lectures descending through him, is not reliable.

"Bro. Gleason was appointed Grand Lecturer of the Grand Lodge of Massachusetts in 1805, and that Grand Lodge appointed no other Grand Lecturer until 1842. He was a liberally educated man; graduated at Brown University in 1802, and was a public lecturer on geography and astronomy. He was a member of Mount Lebanon Lodge, in Massachusetts, in 1807, and died in Concord in that State, in 1847, at the age of 70. He visited England and exemplified the Preston Lectures as he had received them from Bro. Webb, before the Grand Lodge of England, and the Masonic authorities of that Grand Body pronounced them correct. In the year 1817, Bro. John Barney, formerly of Charlotte, Vermont, went to Boston and received the Preston Lectures there as taught by Gleason, and as they were approved by the Grand Lodge of Massachusetts.

"I am unable to say whether he received them from Bro. Gleason himself, or from Bro. Henry Fowle. My impression is that he received them from Bro. Fowle. In possession of these Lectures he returned to Vermont, and at the Annual Communication of our Grand Lodge in October, 1817, visited that Grand Body and made known the fact. The subject was submitted to a committee for examination, which reported that these Lectures were according to the most approved method of Work in the United States, and proposed to give Bro. Barney letters of recommendation to all Lodges and brethren, wherever he may wish to travel, as a brother well qualified to give useful Masonic information to any one who may wish his services.

"The Grand Lodge accepted and adopted the report of its committee, and Bro. Barney, under the recommendation thus given, visited many of the then existing Lodges of this State, and imparted to them a knowledge of these Lectures. Among others, in the year 1818, he visited Dorchester Lodge, in Vergennes, and imparted full instructions in them to Right Worshipful Samuel Wilson, now and for several years past, Grand Lecturer of this State. Upon this occasion Bro. Barney wrote out a portion of them in private key, and Bro. Wilson wrote out the remainder. Both were written in the same book, and that part written by Bro. Wilson was examined carefully and approved by Bro. Barney. That original manuscript is still in existence, and is now in possession of my son, Bro. Philip C. Tucker, Jr., of Galveston, Texas, to whom Bro. Wilson presented it a few years ago. Bro. Wilson has a perfect copy of it, and refers to it as authority in all cases of doubt. Bro. Gallup, of Liberty Lodge, at Franklin, was one of the original Grand Lodge committee, and is still living to attest the correctness and identity of these Lectures as taught by Barney, in 1817.

"These are the only Lectures which have been sanctioned in this jurisdiction, from October, 1817, to the present day. The Grand Lodge has sanctioned no others. My predecessors, Grand Masters Robinson, Whitney, Whales and Haswell, sustained them against all innovations, and to the extent of my power I have done the same. I think upon these facts I am justified in saying that the Lectures we use are the true Lectures of Preston.

"Webb changed the arrangement of the sections as fixed by Preston. For one which he thought more simple and convenient, but, as I understand, he left the body of the Lectures themselves as Preston had established them. Subsequently to 1818, Bro. Barney went to the western and southwestern States; he was a man in feeble health at the time, and pursued Masonic lecturing as a means of subsistence. Upon his return to this State, a few years afterwards, he stated to his brethren here—as I have been credibly informed and believe— that he found different systems of lecturing prevailing at the west and south-west, and that, upon presenting the Lectures he had been taught at Boston in 1817, to different Grand Masters, they were objected to, and that various Grand Masters would not sanction his lecturing in their jurisdictions, unless he would teach the Lectures then existing among them, that desiring to pursue his occultation, he did learn the different systems of lecturing then existing in the different States, and taught them in the different State jurisdictions, as desired by the different Grand Masters in each. This circumstance accounts for the strange disagreement between the east and west and south-west as to what are the true Barney Lectures. They meant one thing in New England and another in the west."

Again, in 1861, he says: "Bro. Gleason was appointed Grand Lecturer of Massachusetts in 1805 and no other Grand Lecturer was appointed by that Grand Lodge until 1842. During all this time Bro. Fowle was a member, sometimes a subordinate officer, and occasionally Master of St. Andrew's Lodge of Boston, one of the oldest and best informed Lodges in the world. For most of this time, also, Bro. Gleason was at home in Massachusetts, and holding his office of Grand Lecturer of his State. Is it not a very violent presumption to assume that he did not know what Lectures and what kind of Work were taught in one of the strongest Lodges of Boston.

"I knew Bro. Henry Fowle from my boyhood. My father was one of his intimate friends, and they were members and officers of the same Charter. Bro. Fowle was a man of far more mind and attainments than are usually found among men of his sphere of life. His was not a mind to forget anything, and was too tenacious a Mason to make changes without authority. But setting all inferences from such considerations aside, I remark, that I was present at St. Andrew's Lodge in 1823 or 1824. AND SAW THE WORK DONE, BRO. FOWLE TAKING PART IN IT THAT EVENING AS A SUBORDINATE OFFICER, AND THE WORK WAS IDENTICALLY THAT WHICH HAS BEEN PRACTICED IN THIS JURISDICTION FROM 1818 TO THIS DAY. AS EXEMPLIFIED IN THE LECTURES COMMUNICATED TO WILSON BY BARNEY. I add also, that I was subjected, upon another occasion, to a thorough examination, in an ante-room of the same Masonic hall, upon a visit to St. Andrew's Chapter, by a strong examining committee, which, finding that I answered readily, ran through the Lectures ENTIRE from entered apprentice to Royal Arch, and that the whole of them were IDENTICAL with those in use in the Lodges and Chapters of Vermont. There can be no doubt, then, that the Lectures communicated by Fowle to Barney were the genuine Lectures taught by Webb and Gleason, the same which Gleason received from Webb in 1801 or 1802; the same which he taught as Grand Lecturer of Massachusetts, from 1805; the same that I found among the Boston Masons, in 1823 or 1824 and the very same which are taught there now.

"Was there any opportunity for them to be falsified in their translation from Barney to Wilson? Barney received them in 1817 and made private notes of them; in October of that year, he submitted them to the Grand Lodge of Vermont, and got its permission to teach them in this jurisdiction: he was well known here, was a man of integrity and had every motive of interest and honor to preserve them in their purity. In 1818 — and before he had gone from the State to teach elsewhere at all — he imparted them to Bro. Wilson, having his original notes before him, and aiding that Brother in making a correct copy of them and when they came into use practically, they were found to exactly agree with those used in the jurisdiction from which Bro. Barney received them. There seems no room for error or mistake here. The link in the chain of transmission is not broken at all."

The work of Webb was evidently well done, and in his life time there existed a fairly uniform method where he or his disciples taught. He died in 1819. Jeremy L. Cross published his *"True Masonic Chart"* in 1819. It was the Webb monitor with the addition of a series of illustrations of the emblems. This feature has been copied in most monitors since.

The "Morgan excitement" in 1826 put Masonic activity to a disadvantage, and there was little done from 1826 to 1839 or thereabouts. Then there was a revival of interest and an agitation for uniform work resulting in the Baltimore Convention of 1843, at which the delegates adopted the "Webb work."

John Barney, of whom Philip Tucker speaks, was made a Mason in Friendship Lodge No. 20, at Charlotte, Vt., in 1811. After teaching the Webb work in Vermont he went west. He was Grand Lecturer in Ohio from 1836 to 1843, and Grand Lecturer of the Grand Lodge of Illinois in 1846 and 1847. He died at Peoria, Ill., June 22, 1847. He was the most influential ritualist of Vermont, Ohio and Illinois. Michigan and Wisconsin, and the states which have since become independent Masonically, derived their work from these, and follow the Barney work to the best of their knowledge.

John Barney was the delegate from Ohio to the Baltimore Convention of 1843. Charles W. Moore of Massachusetts, was also a delegate. In a letter written in 1863 he says:

"The work and lectures of the first three degrees, as adopted and authorized by the Baltimore Convention, in 1843, were, with a few unimportant verbal exceptions, literally as they were originally compiled by Bro. Thos. S. Webb, about the close of the last century, and as they were subsequently taught by him during his lifetime, and also by his early and favorite pupil, Bro. Benjamin Gleason, from the years 1801-2 until his death in 1847. In a note to me, under date of NOV. 25, 1843, Bro. Gleason says: 'It was my privilege while at Brown University, Providence, R.I., (1801-2) to acquire a complete knowledge of the lectures in the first three degrees of Masonry, directly from our late much lamented brother Thos. S. Webb.' In 1805 Bro. Gleason was commissioned by the Grand Lodge of Massachusetts as its Grand Lecturer and empowered to visit and instruct the Lodges in the ritual, as he had received it from Bro. Webb. This duty he performed with great fidelity, and to the entire satisfaction of the Grand Lodge; and this ritual is in use in the lodges of Massachusetts at the present time. There may be some verbal departures from the original, but no material change has been made in it. In 1823-4 Bro. Gleason was my Masonic teacher. I learned the work and lectures of him. We were connected by family ties, and close Masonic relations continued to exist between us until his death in 1847. I was associated with him in all the various branches of Masonry for nearly a quarter of a century, and enjoyed all the rare advantages of his extensive and accurate knowledge of the various rituals of the different grades of the Order. In 1843 I was appointed by the Grand Lodge of Massachusetts a delegate to the Baltimore Masonic Convention, called for the purpose of revising the various modes of work then in use, and agreeing upon a uniform system for the country. Before leaving home, and as a preparation for the better discharge of the duties of the appointment, I availed myself of the assistance of Bro. Gleason, in a thorough and careful revision of the lectures, which I had originally received from him and which, on frequent occasions, I had been called to deliver and work with him, both in-and out of the Lodge. I was, therefore, qualified to report them to the convention, through its committee on the work, in their purity and integrity, and, beyond all doubt, just as they originally came from the hand of the late Bro. Webb. I had the honor to be a member of the committee, and to report the amendments, and the lectures as amended, to the convention. This I did without notes, but subsequently took the precaution-to minute down the alterations from the original; and these are now in my possession. They are mostly verbal, few in number, and not material in their results. The only change of consequence was in the due guards of the second and third degrees, which were changed and made to conform to that of the first degree in position and explanation. This was analogically correct."

At this Baltimore Convention sixteen of the twenty-three then existing Grand Lodges of the United States were represented, and the "work" adopted was called the "National" or "Barney" work. No opposition of consequence to this work occurred until 1860, when Robert Morris tried to have a "Webb-Preston work as taught by Robert Morris" adopted through the medium of a Conservator's Association. This Conservator's Association gained much influence and many brethren lent it their support. The plan was to have a conservator in each lodge who was to use his best efforts to promulgate the "Webb-Preston work as taught by Robert Morris." Each conservator was provided with a copy of "Mnemonics," which Robert Morris claimed was the true work.

The Grand Lodges, however, became alarmed and promptly condemned the Conservators; in the early 60's most of them passed resolutions reaffirming the work as handed down through Gleason, Barney, Wilson, Wadsworth, Cross and others, and as approved and recommended by the Baltimore Convention. Robert Morris claimed to have received the work from Bro. Wilson of Vermont; but Bro. Wilson says:

"In 1857 Robert Morris visited Vermont for the purpose of ascertaining what were the true Webb lectures. P. C. Tucker introduced Morris to me for the purpose, and I loaned him a copy (not my original) of my cipher, and which unfortunately had several omissions through mistake. In copying this, Morris made several mistakes and misread many passages. In fact he could never read it at all until I met him in Chicago in 1860, and I think he cannot read it all now. This copy, with its blunders and omissions, is the text from which the book you refer to (Mnemonics) was made."

If we are correct in judging the condition which prevailed from 1843, when the Baltimore Convention was held, until the time of the Conservator's Association, we would conclude that there was a difference in the work in the different Jurisdictions which made a Conservator movement possible. (6)

Robert Morris may have been sincerely desirous of promoting a uniform work and believed he could accomplish it; He probably could if he had possessed either the Preston work or the Webb work, but he had neither. His was a Morris work, and there had been too many changes to suit the Brethren, and from then until now the work adopted and maintained in the East and Northwest (7) has been as near the Webb work as our ritualists could ascertain, with the exception of Pennsylvania which still adheres to the "Ancient" work.

NOTES:

(1) See Mackey's Enc., Article Lectures, for simple questions and answers.

(2) See Hutchinson's "Spirit of Masonry."

(3) History of Freemasonry and Concordant Orders, by Hughan, page 250.

(4) A considerable difference of opinion exists as to what was done. See "Hughan's English Royal Arch." "Sadler's Reprints and Revelations."

(5) We think this a rather improbable claim, as Bro. Cross was not made a Mason until 1808.

(6) "Two text books, differing materially were issued, each claiming to be the work adopted. (By the Baltimore convention). I have heard a dozen variations of the lectures, each declared to be such as were agreed upon at Baltimore." A. T. C. Pierson, G. M., Minn., 1858.

(7) I am uninformed as to the South and Southwest.

THE MEANING OF INITIATION
by Frank C. Higgins

In all ancient rites and mysteries the participants in which were received by initiation, the greatest care was always exercised with respect to certain details, which if not properly carried out might mar or invalidate the entire ceremony.

The true significance of all initiation has ever been that of a spiritual rebirth. The sacred Agrouchada of the Hindus says, "The first birth is merely the advent into material life; the second birth is the entrance to a spiritual life."

The newly initiated into the first degree of Brahmanism was called *douidja*, which means "twice born." The very word initiate indicates that the candidate is at least symbolically in the same situation as if he had had no previous existence. He is to be ushered into an altogether new world.

In ancient initiations the extremity of humility was expressed by the rent garments of contrition for past offenses in the life about to be blotted out, the bosom offered to the executioner's sword, and the attitude of a captive.

PREPARING THE CANDIDATE

The most curious custom perhaps had to do with what might be termed the complete preparation of the candidate against the influences that had affected his previous career. During the multitude of centuries in the course of which astrology was thought to play the strongest part in human affairs, every circumstance affecting the welfare of humanity was deemed to have its rise in one or another of the planets, or perhaps in a lucky or evil combination of several. The science of medicine rose entirely from this curious belief in planetary affinities. The ancient physician diagnosed his patient's malady according to the diseases listed under the latter's unlucky stars and tried to cure it by application of substances designated as governed by those planets favorable to him. The same idea governed the individual with reference to articles carried upon his person. The superstitious carried various charms and amulets intended to draw favorable planetary influences to his aid, and was just as careful to avoid substance that might produce a contrary effect.

In the ordering of the candidate for initiation into the ancient mysteries this belief played an important part. The candidate might carry upon his person nothing that would invite the attention of occult planetary powers through the mysterious tie that bound them to terrestrial objects.

METALLIC TOKENS

The lists of plants, flowers, minerals, metals, and other things that were subject to these mysterious influences were long and complicated. Gold linked him with the sun which incited to the besetting sin of intellectual pride; silver drew upon him the fickle qualities of the moon; copper, sacred to Venus, provoked lust, and iron, the metal of Mars, quarrelsomeness; tin, tyranny and oppression, the qualities of Jupiter; lead, sloth and indolence, belonging to Saturn; while mercury or quicksilver was responsible for dishonesty and covetousness. Therefore a key or a coin, and above all a sword, was likely to bring confusion upon the whole mysterious operation of regeneration.

Above all were enjoined upon the candidate the three sacred virtues, which by the Jain sects in India are still called "the three jewels," represented by three circles, "right belief," "right knowledge," and "right conduct." In order to reach the spiritual plane, in which the soul is entirely freed from the bonds of matter, these were the chief necessities, and the person who clung to them would certainly go higher until he reached the state of liberation.

THREE REGULAR STEPS

To the ancient candidate were also recommended "the three successive steps which open the soul to free and unobstructed activity and communication on both the psychic and the spiritual planes." The first was to still the ego and empty the mind of every bias and standard of self and sense. The second consisted, when this passive state had been induced, in fixing and holding the attention upon the specific object about which the truth was desired.

Thirdly, the foregoing two steps having been taken, the individual was to stand firmly and persistently in the receptive and listening attitude for the immediate revelation of the truth, in the full expectation of getting it. This receptive state and expectant attitude opened the consciousness to "the psychic vibrations that write unerringly their story on the receptive mind."

WHOM DOES THE CANDIDATE REPRESENT?

Within the simple and easily formulated problem asked in the heading is contained the sublimest of all secrets, which various of the higher degrees have sought to answer, each in its own way. It involves the intimate application of all the symbolic degrees to the initiate himself, without which they are as empty as air.

In all the ancient mysteries a character was assumed by the candidate, and as the candidates were any and the character depicted always the same, it must have represented something essentially common to all alike. Furthermore, the precise similarity of the experiences to which each individual candidate was subjected argued the identical lesson in all cases.

Examination of all available detail, especially the sacred writings of many races, confirms us in the conviction that this universal character was but an allegorical representation of the ego or "self," engaged in the warfare of which it has been said that the victor is greater than he who taketh a city" and emerging a conqueror in the very instant of apparent defeat. We receive our earliest concrete presentation of such a character in the celebrated document known as the *Egyptian Book of the Dead*, the Bible of the builders of the Pyramids, fragments of which are found wrapped in the cloths of almost every mummy.

THE PILGRIM SOUL

The Book of the Dead presents the wanderings of a departed soul through the underworld to the council of the gods, who were to listen to its accusers, give heed to its defenders, and finally weigh its accumulated good deeds in the scales against the feather symbol of "truth." The name of this character is given as Ani the Scribe. It finally transpired that this name was equivalent to the Latin term ego, meaning the "I Am" or "self" in man. This leads to what was perhaps the greatest and most important of all secret teachings of the ancient world, one that has become so obscured by the confusion of its many dramatic representations with real historical characters, — that most clear and careful labor is required to trace the main ideas from age to age and people to people, in order to show that they are fundamentally everywhere exactly the same.

There is no difficulty whatever in recognizing the self-conscious principle in every man as being an actual spark of the infinite self-consciousness precipitated into material existence, through the labyrinth of which it is compelled to strive in ceaseless search for the Master's Word, the secret of its being and immortal destiny. If this idea of the struggle of a divine and immortal soul, weighed down with the burden of matter and assailed at every turn by foes that symbolize the continual transformations of matter from "life" to "death" and "death" to "life," be taken as the vital principle of every drama of regeneration, from the *"Book of the Dead"* to John Bunyan's *"Pilgrim Progress,"* we too shall have progressed a long way upon the road to understanding that of Freemasonry.

THE PILOT STAR

The beautiful star that is the chief emblem of the Royal Arch degree, besides being the sacred symbol of Israel, has had no other meaning during the thousands of years from the most ancient Brahmanism to the Temple of today. Even when called "the United Seal of Vishnu and Siva," the "Immortal" and the "Mortal," or "Fire" the symbol of Spirit, and "Water" the symbol of Matter, it represented the same idea, that of the "Self Conqueror," the Perfect Man, who had learned the subjugation of human passions and perfection in attitude toward God and fellow man. Thus the uppointing triangle stood for the ascent of matter into spirit which is typified by the phrase "resurrection of the body," and the down-pointing triangle the descent of spirit into matter, and the complete star represents the immortal being fitted to dwell in "that house not built with hands, eternal in the heavens."

THE DOCTRINE OF THE BALANCE
by Joseph Fort Newton

Readers of Albert Pike will recall the stately pages with which *Morals and Dogma* closes, setting forth, in a manner unforgettable, the Doctrine of the Balance. Many had taught this truth before time out of mind, no one more impressively than the man whom Pike was richly indebted, (1) but his exposition is none the less his own. With vast labor he brings together his findings, showing that to this result the wisdom of the ages runs, what the sages have thought equally with what the mystics have dreamed. Always it is a triad, suggested by the ancient idea of the number Three, the singular, the dual and the plural, the odd and even added, and the great emblem of the Triangle — symbol of perfection. It is seen in all Masonic symbolism, from end to end and at every step of the Mystic quest for the secret which every Mason is seeking.

Eloquently, and with every variation of emphasis and illustration, he lays the matter before us, carrying it into all the fields of human activity and aspiration. Sympathy and Antipathy, Attraction and Repulsion, Fate and Freedom, each a fact of life and a force of nature, are contraries alike in the universe and in the soul of man, wherein we see eternity in miniature. As the earth is held in its orbit by the action of opposing forces, so truth is made up of two opposite propositions, as peace lies in the union of motion and rest, and harmony is the fruit of seeming war. Here he finds the solution of the problem of the One and the Many, of the Infinite and the Finite, of Unity amidst Manifoldness: the principle of the Balance, the secret of the universal equilibrium:

"Of that Equilibrium in the Deity, between the Infinite Divine Wisdom and the Infinite Divine Power; from which result the Stability of the Universe, the unchangeableness of the Divine Law, and the Principles of Truth, Justice, and Right which are a part of it; . . Of that Equilibrium also, between the Infinite Divine Justice and the Infinite Divine Mercy, the result of which is the Infinite Divine Equity, and the Moral Harmony or Beauty of the Universe. By it the endurance of created and imperfect natures in the presence of a Perfect Deity is made possible.

Of that Equilibrium between Necessity and Liberty, between the action of the Divine Omnipotence and the Free-will of man, by which vices and base actions, and ungenerous thoughts and words are crimes and wrongs, justly punished by the law of cause and consequence, though nothing in the universe can happen or be done contrary to the will of God; and without which co-existence of Liberty and Necessity, of Free-will in the creature and Omnipotence in the Creator, there could be no religion, nor any law of right and wrong, or merit or demerit, nor any justice in human punishments or penal laws.

And, finally, of that Equilibrium, possible in ourselves, and which Masonry incessantly labors to accomplish in its Initiates, and demands of its Adepts and Princes (else unworthy of their titles between the Spiritual and Divine and the Material and human in man; between the Intellect, Reason, and Moral Sense on one side, and the Appetites and Passions on the other, from which result the Harmony and Beauty of a well-regulated life." (2) And so on, through a passage of singular elevation both of language and of thought, we are led by an ancient truth which becomes a vision in the mind of a nobler thinker. My design is not to add to his exposition, but to apply it with emphasis and illustration, if so that it may be brought home to our "business and bosom" and be of real service to us in the life which we live together, and in the life which each must live alone. For it is the high service of Masonry that it puts a man in the straight path which the wisest of the race have walked, leading him midway between the falsehood of extremes, and bringing the highest teaching of the past to the uses of the present. After all, how to live is the one matter; and he is wise who joins the goodly Shakespeare gospel of Courage, Sanity and Pity with that other Gospel of Faith, Hope, and Love. Every man will need all the aid he can get, unless he be content, as no real man can be, to live in the world as a mere looker-on at a drama in which others are actors.

"In God's vast house a curious guest, Seeing how all works take their flight."

From bottom to top life is a contradiction and a paradox, and the beginning of wisdom is to know that fact and adjust ourselves to it. Light and darkness, heat and cold, mind and matter, fate and free-will, asceticism and indulgence, socialism and anarchy, dogmatism and doubt, reason and authority — no man may ever hope to live long enough, much less to think deeply enough, to harmonize these paradoxes. The way of wisdom is to accept both facts in each case, as the Two Pillars of a Temple of Truth, and walk between them into the hush of the holy place. Either one, without the other, is only a half-truth which ends in perversion, if not in insanity, turning the hearty, wholesome, clear seeing spirit of manhood into the pitiful narrowness and hardness of a bigot or a fanatic.

For example: "All is free- that is false: all is fate — that is false. All things are free and fated — that is true." (3) It is possible to make an argument in behalf of fatalism so freezing that one is left with the feeling that he is no more responsible for his thoughts and acts, than he is for the shape of his head and the color of his eyes. Having listened to such an argument, each of us may say, as Dr. Johnson did, (4) "I know I am free, and that's the end on it." On the other side, one can present a thesis in proof of the freedom of man so convincing that fate seems a fiction. Both are true, and the great truth consists of two opposites which are not contradictory — that it is the Fate of man to be Free if he fights for it, approves himself worthy of it, uniting his will with the Will of the Master of the World! Otherwise, we men are slaves journeying downward "to the dust of graves," slaves of greed and passion and a fatal folly.

Asceticism is one extreme, indulgence another. One would repress every natural instinct in behalf of a pale, wan purity; the other would follow every fancy, driven hither and yon by every gust of passion, at the mercy of every caprice. Between the two lies temperance, keeping the balance between two absurdities, making a right use of everything, and abusing nothing; its motto the wise words of the old Greeks, "In nothing too much." Socialism seems to hold that the State is everything, the Individual nothing — or at best only a cog in a vast machine, an atom in an indistinguishable blur. Anarchy makes the State nothing, and the Individual everything — each a law unto himself, and chaos at the end. Between the two lies the way of wise government in which "Freedom slowly broadens down from precedent to precedent," or grows gladly up from the life of a just and intelligent people. There are certain things which every man must surrender in behalf of the common good, and other things which it were a sin to abdicate, the while a shifting, zig-zag line runs between dividing the man from the mass.

By the same token, in religion Dogmatism affirms everything, makes a map of the Infinite, and an atlas of Eternity, so certain is it of things whereof no man knoweth. It talks of God as if He were a man in the next room. It knows the origin of all things, and the final destiny of humanity. Doubt denies everything, questions the competence of the human mind to know Divine things, leaving us with the assurance that nothing is certain but uncertainty; nothing secure but insecurity. Again it is the doctrine of the balance, as in the natural world peace is found amid the poise of powers. Between dogmatism and doubt is a wise and reverent Faith, which dares to say, "Now we know in part — a tiny part, no doubt — but knowledge is real as far as it goes, and what we know gives us confidence in the vast Unknown. And so we make bold to trust the ultimate decency of things and the veiled kindness of the Father of men, assured that He who has brought us to where we are will lead us to where we ought to be!"

Of this fundamental paradox of life the Cross is the symbol. Older than Christianity, as old, almost, as human life, it is the supreme symbol of the race. When man first emerged from the "old dark backward and abysm of time," he had a cross in his hand. Where he got it, what he meant by it, many may conjecture but no one knows. The Cross, like life itself, is also a collision and a contradiction — its four arms pointing every whither, making it the great guide-post of free thought. As long as a man keeps his poise, never forgetting the profound paradox at the heart of all high thought, he may think as far and as fast as his mind can go. For many of us, of course, the Cross is hallowed anew and forever by the name of One whose life was a tragedy, whose love was heroic in its gentleness, who wins by "that strange power called weakness," whose character is the sovereign wonder of the world, and whose spirit is the holiest tradition of humanity.

Since this is so, since the way of sanity, if not of salvation, lies in keeping our balance, why is it that men lose their poise ? No man of us, when he thinks of the days agone, but recalls acts which he not only regrets, but which puzzle him by their strange stupidity. He would give almost as much to be able to understand them as he would to forget them. Why is this so? Shakespeare has much to teach us here, much of abiding profit to remember, if so that we may understand the past and make a better use of the future. He everywhere shows that tragedy is the fruit of treachery, and that treachery has its roots in obsession (5) — some one thing that gets so close to the mind that it can see nothing else, blinds it, preys upon it, making a man first a fanatic, and then, it may be, a criminal. Macbeth was a man of noble nature; his wife was a lovely lady. They became obsessed with ambition for place and power, and to what dark depths of sin and shame that mad blindness led them that terrible tragedy tells us. This lesson, taught so often by our supreme poet, is for each of us, teaching us to keep our poise, and to flee an obsession as a plague. Whatever fastens itself upon the mind, shutting out the light, marring the proportions and perspectives of things, forebodes disaster.

Perhaps it is physical passion. If so, it will turn love into lust and make the world a bawdy-house. It may be political ambition, and a man throws everything to the winds in order to win, forgetting that no office on earth is worth the sacrifice of integrity — and, also, if he wins by trickery he is unfit to hold it. It may be religion. Think of the crimes unspeakable, the brutalities unbelievable, which have been committed by men in a frenzy of fanatical bigotry — dipping their hands in blood and thinking they were doing the will of God ! They were madmen. Plato said that all men are more or less insane, and that the man whom we put in a straightjacket is only a little more emphatically out of his mind than the rest of us. The more reason, then, why we should keep our poise and walk the quiet way of sanity and charity, in love of God and man.

After this manner we expound the Doctrine of the Balance, as taught by Pike, reminding our Brethren, as we remind ourselves, that the wisdom of life lies in freedom, serenity, and forgiveness, in victory by selfsurrender to the highest laws of life, and that we dare not turn either to the right or the left. By such teaching men become happy and free; in this way we may grow old without being sad, and wise without being cynical; and learn, at last, that everlasting gentleness which is the highest wisdom man may win from the hard facts and the often strange medley of his days. Let us also lay to heart the prayer quoted by Pike:

"Let Him, the ever-living God, be always present in thy mind; for thy mind itself is His likeness, for it, too, is invisible and impalpable, and with out form. As He exists forever, so thou also, when thou shalt put off this which is visible and corruptible, shalt stand before Him forever, living and endowed with knowledge."

NOTES:

(1) Eliphas Levi. *Digest of his Writings*, translated by A.E. Waite, especially pp. 79-83.

(2) *Morals and Dogma*, pp. 859-60.

(3) *Life of F.W. Robertson*, p. 32, note.

(4) *Life of Johnson*, by Boswell.

(5) *Shakespeare*, by John Masefield.

OPERATIVE MASONRY:
EARLY DAYS IN THE MASONIC ERA
by Robert I. Clegg

We Masons deem Masonry as being peculiarly religious, some Masons indeed being quoted to the effect that in their judgment Masonry is a religion. Who of us but at some time has heard of a brother in his enthusiasm saying "Masonry is a good enough religion for me"? But Masonry itself makes no such claim. At best it stands as the handmaid of religion, in all lands and among all faiths earnestly supporting and serving those accepted convictions of morality in which all good men agree.

As was shown in the paper prepared for the November issue of the Bulletin of the National Masonic Research Society there was a time when in the church and outside these sacred precincts the craftsmen of old gave freely of their money, their numbers, and in fact of all their opportunities to advance the cause of the prevailing religion. It is only fair to suppose that in all other matters these workmen were equally advanced and aggressive. Some of these angles of their organizations and of their methods will be taken up in the present paper.

Perhaps a word or two of special explanation is necessary at this stage. I am dealing with a period when many bodies of workmen copied each other's practices. For one reason of this similarity there was the common source of authority from whence they derived their characters. The Government gave them liberty to proceed for similar objects and in the attainment of these purposes they would no doubt find it very desirable in meeting all the requirements of the law to follow in each other's footsteps. Thus the associations of carpenters, of ironworkers, of goldsmiths, of tanners, as well as of Masons and the other societies, had like officers and laws. Such little differences as crept in were occasioned by the inevitable problems incident to each trade and profession and the successive adjustments of them that periodically called for attention and settlement.

The general construction of these bodies and their operation was known as the gild system. Common to all the recognized trades approved by the Government we can examine it as the exemplar of our own fraternity though Masonry was but one branch of it. I am also of opinion that Masonry has an earlier origin though at this moment I shall not venture into this far distant field of investigation and controversy.

The various crafts were often termed "the mysteries." Subject to the same city and national government it frequently happened that the laws enacted for their control shed much light upon the purposes of the societies and the manner in which they were regarded by the citizens at large.

An old ordinance of the city of London provided suitable punishment for those who were "rebellious, contradictory, or fractious" against the Masters of the Mysteries "that so such persons may not duly perform their duties." The preliminary part of the same enactment throws light upon the purpose of these early craft organizations.

"Item, it is ordained that all the mysteries of the city of London shall be lawfully regulated and governed, each according to its nature in due manner, that so no knavery, false workmanship, or deceit, shall be found in any manner in the said mysteries; for the honor of the good folks of the said mysteries, and for the common profit of the people. And in each mystery there shall be chosen and sworn four or six, or more or less, according as the mystery shall need; which persons, so chosen and sworn, shall have full power from the Mayor well and lawfully to do and to perform the same."

Then follow a series of fines and terms of imprisonment for such as "shall thereof be attained" of interfering with the carrying out of the above plan of craft administration.

Why would the city take so direct an interest in the control of the crafts, you may ask. If so careful a supervision and recognition of the situation is taken then is it not likely that the very same fount of authority would have something to say as to the manner in which the members as well as their officers may be selected?

You may also rightfully infer that the city then held something of the same relationship to the several crafts as is now occupied by the Grand Lodges. Such would appear to have been the case in very large measure. Consider if you please the following ordinance which accompanies the one just quoted in reference to the obedience and respect due to the Masters of mysteries:

"Also, because as well in times past, out of memory, as also in modern times, the city aforesaid is wont to be defended and governed by the aid and counsels as well as of the reputable men of the trades-merchant as of the other trades-handicraft; and from of old it hath been the usage, that no strange person, native or alien, as to whose conversation and condition there is no certain knowledge, shall be admitted to the freedom of city, unless first, the merchants or traders of the city following the trade which the person so to be admitted intends to adopt, shall be lawfully convoked, that so, by such his fellow citizens, so convoked, the Mayor and Aldermen aforesaid, being certified as to the condition and trustworthiness of the persons so to be admitted, may know whether such persons ought to be admitted or rejected; the whole community demands, that the form aforesaid, so far as concerns the more important trades and handicrafts, shall in future be in violably observed, that so no person in future may against the provision aforesaid be admitted to the freedom of the city."

What Mason worth the name but will say with all his heart that it were well for us now that in selecting material for membership the choice should always be made in a manner to insure the obtaining of those persons upon whom the community may well rely for counsel, for defense, or for government.

Here and there in traversing the directions found in these early ordinances of the gilds we find a glimmer at least by which light has been borrowed for the thoughtful Masons of the present day in making their explanations of various oldtime customs. Who, for instance, has not wondered at that secret that could not be given in the absence of one of the three possessors?

Years ago in a foreign land I went as a boy with my grandfather to the meeting of a trade organization of which he was treasurer. The official chest of the society caught my eye. It contained books and papers as well as other valuables of which I knew little or nothing. These did not particularly interest me. What did attract my especial attention was the fact that the box was secured by three locks. Why three when one was ample for such security as appeared necessary? But it was explained to me that the three keys were in the possession of each of three responsible officers of the organization and that the box could not then be opened unless these three officers with their respective keys were present.

Such a custom is very old. In the reign of Edward II of England, 1307-1327, there was passed an ordinance by the City Fathers of London that "Also, it was demanded that the common seal should remain in future in a certain chest under six locks; of which locks three Alderman should have three keys, and certain reputable men of the Commonalty the three other keys."

That a candidate for Freemasonry shall himself be a free agent is well known and is most desirable. We go further and require him to be freeborn. This does not appear to be a universal demand made of the initiate as in England, for example, the requirement is that he be a "freeman." There is an obvious distinction between the two and our practice in this country substantially exacts that both conditions shall exist.

Here, again, the matter is of very old usage. "For avoiding disgrace and scandal unto the city of London" it was ordained in 1389 "that from henceforth no foreigner shall be enrolled as an apprentice, or be received unto the freedom of the said city by way of apprenticeship, unless he shall first make oath that he is a freeman and not a bondman. And whoever shall hereafter be received unto the freedom of the said city, by purchase or in any other way than by apprenticeship, shall make the same oath, and shall also find six reputable citizens of the said city, who shall give security for him, as such from of old hath been wont to be done.

"And if it shall so happen that any such bondman is admitted unto the freedom of the said city upon a false suggestion, the Chamberlain being ignorant thereof, immediately after it shall have become notorious unto the Mayor and Alderman that such person is a bondman, he shall lose the freedom of the city and shall pay a fine for such his deceit at the discretion of the Mayor and Alderman, saving always such liberty as pertains unto the soil of the said franchise.

"Also, if it shall happen in future, and may it not so chance, that such bondman, a person, that is to say, at the time of whose birth his father was a bondman, is elected to judicial rank in the said city, that of Alderman, for example, Sheriff, or Mayor; unless before receiving such promotion, he shall notify unto the Mayor and Alderman such his servile condition, he shall pay unto the Chamberlain one hundred pounds, to the use of the city, and nevertheless shall lose the freedom, as already stated."

Riley in his edition of the "Liber Albus," the "White Book" of the city of London, further points out some qualifications of the Aldermen of the gild epoch which have an interest in our present study. Says he, "High honor was paid to the Aldermen in ancient times. Indeed, no person was accepted as Alderman unless he was free from deformity in body, wise and discreet in mind, rich, honest, trustworthy, free, and on no account of low or servile condition; lest perchance the disgrace or opprobrium that might be reflected upon him by reason of his birth, might have the additional effect of casting a slur upon the other Alderman and the whole city as well. And hence it is that from of old no one was made apprentice, or at all events admitted to the freedom of the said city, unless he was known to be of free condition."

Contained in the Liber Albus is the oath of the Masters and Wardens of the mysteries. This I transcribe. It will be noticed that there is left a blank for the filling in of the name of the organization to which the testifying officials are accredited.

"You shall swear, that well and lawfully you shall overlook the art or mystery of . . . of which you are Masters, or Wardens, for the year elected. And the good rules and ordinances of the same mystery, approved here by the Court, you shall keep and cause to be kept. And all the defaults that you shall find therein, done contrary thereto, you shall present unto the Chamberlain of the city, from time to time, sparing no one for favor, and aggrieving no one for hate. Extortion or wrong unto no one, by color of your office, you shall do; nor unto anything that shall be against the estate and peace of the King, or of the city, you shall consent. But for the time that you shall be in office, in all things pertaining unto the said mystery, according to the good laws and franchises of the said city, well and lawfully you shall behave yourself. So God you help, and the Saints."

These citations from the legal enactments of the time do not convey all that could and should be said of the middle ages. That is the era from whence we Masons have drawn so freely of inspiration, of ceremonial, and even of phraseology. Romantic were the industrial activities. From the candlestick upon the altar to the pinnacle of the lofty spire reaching high toward heaven, in the buildings of that day and especially the structures housing the worshippers of God, everything was done in the devotion of a simple straightforward truth of workmanship, a practical genius for constructional invention, the practice of a craft direct, faithful and self-respecting.

Says Batchelder: "It was once the glory of art to be of service. It is difficult for us to fully realize the spirit of an age when art was actually practiced by a great mass of people; when carvers in stone and wood, workers in iron, textile weavers, potters, goldsmiths, found daily opportunity and incentive to bring invention to bear upon their problems, to apply creative thought to the work of their hands. It was a time when builders were architects; when workmen were designers; when contracts called for nothing more than sound materials and honest workmanship, - the art was thrown in as a matter of course."

And he further gives us an illuminating insight of the conditions by which these workmen were trained. "The training received by the mediaeval craftsman was peculiar to the gild system of the time. Many of the masters whose names are familiar to us now in our study of the history of art were duly apprenticed to a craft as soon as they could read, write, and count. Often at an age of ten years they went to the home of the master workman, with whom their apprenticeship was to be served, where as was the custom of the time, they lived. The years of apprenticeship were years of hard work, often of drudgery; but in the great variety of commissions undertaken by the shops of the time an opportunity was presented to lend a hand at many interesting tasks. There seems to have been a spirit of cooperation among the various shops and workmen that the keen relentless competition of modern times does not permit.

"After serving his apprenticeship a lad became a companion or journeyman worker, and finally tried for his degree, if it may be so termed, by submitting to an examination for the title of master workman. In this examination he was called upon not only to produce his masterpiece, but to fashion such tools of his craft as were necessary for its completion. The standards of the gilds were so high that to become a master meant the production of a piece of work satisfactory to the judges artistically as well as technically. This completed the education of a craftsman of the time, producing a workman who was encouraged at every step of his training to combine beauty with utility, technical skill with honest workmanship."

Further on in speaking of the versatility of the old craftsmen, he proceeds: "When they in turn became master workmen, we know not whether to call them goldsmiths or bronze workers, carvers or sculptors, painters or architects, for their training was such that they could turn their hands to any of these with distinction. Orcagna could build a church, cut the stone, lay the mosaics, paint the frescoes, or carve the crucifix, and we know not where most to admire him. While Ghilerti was engaged in the production of the bronze doors for the Florentine baptistry, his journeymen were seldom so early at the foundry but that they found him there in his cap and apron. Brunelleschi watched the building of the cathedral from his bench long before he dreamed that it would be his part to crown it with its great dome; and when he and Donatello went to Ptome to study the antique, they replenished their empty purses by following their craft. What manner of architects were these who went to the quarries and picked out their own stones, who superintended the construction, directed the erection of scaffolds, who could teach others how to lay the mosaics or carve the ornament; and during leisure intervals wrote sonnets, built bridges, planned forts, and invented weapons of defense? When a master received a commission to build a church, a municipal palace, a fountain, or what not, he took with him his own journeymen and apprentices; and when the commission was an important one, he gathered about him to cooperate, in a spirit that knew little of rivalry or jealousy, the best master workers of his day."

From this excellent description of the craft in the gild days much may be conjectured of the progress by which Masonry has become what it is today. To some of these angles of discussion I shall later return. That in the Craft there grew up a method of perpetuating the instruction slowly gained by the masters is only to be expected. These secrets of the trade would only be confided to the safe depositories of faithful breasts.

Geometry and symbolism would be as they are now employed by expert designers for practically laying out their work. To me the mosaic pavement always suggests the cross-sectioned paper of the engineer. To me every symbol is an aid to the memory. All there is of Masonry breathes the craft soul of cooperative labor, the means and the machinery to impress upon the receptive mind lessons of moral and physical importance.

We cannot in one such paper as the foregoing connect the middle ages with the transition period marked off for us by the Grand Lodge era ushered in by the celebrated union of 1717.

Neither can we say much if anything now of that far earlier period of these geometrical builders of the Egyptian temples and pyramids, or of the Roman Collegia with its trades union methods, or of the mysteries of Greece and other lands. All have a bearing of much consequence upon our own fraternity.

Freemasonry has inherited by a long line of descent a philosophy and a nomenclature, a ceremonial system, the outgrowth of innumerable heads of the wisest, and of hearts most devoted. Love and wisdom has been showered upon it in abundance. Years of many centuries have dignified it. A hale and useful age for it claims unbounded respect. Service is its purpose, betterment its aim.

Even as the craftsmen of the past loved their craft, and through its medium turned rawest materials into forms of imperishable beauty, so were they cautious in their materials of membership, selecting them wisely and in their choice and government practicing such methods as were approved by civic and national authorities. Yea, so are we compelled by our profession to be equally discreet and skilful. By the correct selection and perfection of every element in the structure do we build aright the edifice Masonic.

NOTES FOR FURTHER RESEARCH UPON OPERATIVE MASONRY

The "Liber Albus" is a compilation from the archives of the city of London. Its references are of date prior to the year 1419. A translation from its original text in Latin and Anglo-Norman was made by Henry T. Riley and published by Richard Griffin and Co. in 1861. Occasionally found in public libraries but is now out of print and only to be purchased through those tireless bibliophiles, the book-hunters of Masonry. My dear friend, the late Scott Bonham, once urged his readers to buy the "Liber Albus" but at that time he was not aware that it was out of usual trade circles and only to be reached through old-book dealers.

My references to Batchelder are to his delightful treatise on "Design in Theory and Practice," published by the Macmillan Co. of New York, London, and Toronto. I quote the 1910 edition.

A most charming book on the gilds is that of the "Gilds and Companies of London" by George Unwin, and published by Methuen and Co., 36 Essex street, W.C., London. From this work I have not borrowed but my essay would have been much improved if I had had occasion to freely quote from Mr. Unwin. His work lends itself more aptly to another paper I have in mind. At present I need only call attention to several points of importance. First there is an excellent bibliographical list from which many references can be drawn to what material may be obtainable in your local libraries or for purchase from the book dealers. In the preface is an outline that may profitably be followed in the study of the gild system not only in Great Britain but on the continent. My Unwin has among his several chapters one dealing with a class of gilds that were neither merchant nor handicraft. Of such was the English Gild of Knights. There was also in France the organization for the preservation of peace, La Commune de la Paix. In purpose and in practice this association strongly resembled the body that provides the legend for the grade of Patriarch Noachite.

I have not quoted from the "Hole Craft and Fellowship of Masons." This book published in 1894 is, I understand, practically off the market. My own copy was secured through the author, Bro. Edward Conder, Jr. In London the book was published by Swan, Sonnenschein and Company, and in New York by Macmillan and Co. In the introduction Bro. Conder says: "The Worshipful Company of Masons of the City of London enjoys, beside the interest attached to it on account of its antiquity and continuity, the peculiar distinction, above all other gilds, of being one of the principal connecting links in that chain of evidence which proves that the modern social cult, known as the Society of Free and Accepted Masons, is lineally descended from the old Fraternity of Masons which flourished in the early days of monastic architecture, now known by the inappropriate title of Gothic. The history of this Company will I think conclusively prove that the traditions and moral teachings of the old Fellowship which undoubtedly existed in Britain in the 12th and 13th centuries, were preserved by the Masons Company of London, after the downfall of the Church, in 1530, until the middle of the 17th century - at which period non-operative masons and others carried on the old Society with considerable energy, their participation culminating, in 1717, in the establishment of a Grand Lodge, and the subsequent rapid formation of Lodges in all parts of the country." Maybe I shall later return to an examination of the evidence by which Bro. Conder proposes to prove his point. It was with such a thought in mind that I purposely refrained from using on this occasion his temptingly quotable volume.

"The Cathedral Builders" by Leader Scott is also not a readily obtainable book. For my own choice I can get along very well with a substitute, "The Comacines, Their Predecessors and Their Successors." Written by Bro. W. Ravenscroft in most readable style - its brevity is the only fault I can see in it. The publisher is Elliot Stock, 62 Paternoster Row, E.C., London. Bro. Ravenscroft shows the symbols of the Comacines have a pertinent interest to Freemasons, as in the case of the lion, the knot of Solomon, the cable tow, etc.

In Mackey's Encyclopedia, published by the Masonic History Co. of New York, look up the following references: Mysteries, Ancient; Osiris, Mysteries of; Egyptian Mysteries; Cabiric Mysteries; Orphic Mysteries; Cavern; Essenes; Comacines; Druses; Druidical Mysteries; Culdees; Chaldeans; Roman Colleges of Artificers; Gilds; Cologne, Charter of; Crusades; Oath of the Gild; Stone Masons of the Middle Ages; Strict Observance; Hund, Baron von; etc.

The *Ars Coronatorum* or transactions of the Quatuor Coronati Lodge of London have scattered through their scholarly pages much of the keenest degree of interest in this line of investigation. A complete index is very desirable. The series of volumes is also very rare. Stray copies and partial sets are occasionally to be obtained. My reference to the practical use of the mosaic pavement in laying out a building is borne out by a paper in the "Ars" by Sir Caspar Purden Clarke whose experience in the Orient enabled him to see this method actually employed by the Eastern workmen.

My brother engineers may be also interested in the fact that in an interview with the famous builders of bridges, Gustave Lindenthal, he explained the probable method by which the early builders managed to design safe constructions for their remarkably daring edifices, aqueducts and so forth. At that time the structural analysis by mathematical means was of course not so developed as at the present day. A method whereby weights suspended by cords; a sort of inverted balance, probably gave the early builders practical foothold for finding the direction and amount of the forces to be withstood by their structures. Such methods and the general system of proportions for buildings in common use were doubtless transmitted secretly to pupils and sworn associates. Here would be another means for the mutual protection and also for profitable prominence to clients of the craftsmen.

My few suggestions above are by no means intended to exhaust all the sources of information on this subject. There are many others and I do not pretend to have enumerated what some of my brethren will consider obvious and of consequence. But as I shall come back to this topic, and as I hope to deal then with matters mentioned in certain of the foregoing references I take the opportunity of calling attention to them now.

MASONIC JURISPRUDENCE
by Roscoe Pound

At the outset we may well ask ourselves why do we say Masonic Juris-prudence? Why not simply Masonic Law ? Is there a science of Masonic law as distinct from Masonic law itself? For in its original and etymological meaning and in the best usage, jurisprudence means the science of law. It is true there are two other uses of the term. The French use it to mean the course of decision in the courts as contrasted on the one hand with legisla-tion and on the other hand with doctrine or the consensus of opinion of learned writers and commentators. To some extent this French usage has been received with us, particularly in the phrase "equity jurisprudence," signifying the course of decision in Anglo-American courts of equity, which has gained currency through the classical work of Judge Story. But it must be obvious that Masons do not employ the word in this sense. Although the course of decision in Masonic tribunals in the form of rulings of the Grand Masters and action of Grand Lodges thereon and of review of trials in or by Grand Lodges, is an important form of Masonic law; it furnishes but a part, and relatively a modern part, of the materials of what we are wont to style Masonic jurisprudence.

By a not unnatural transition from the French use of the term it has come to be used also chiefly in this country, simply as a polysyllabic syn-onym for law. Medical jurisprudence, for the forensic applications of medi-cine, has much vogue. Dental jurisprudence for the law of interest to den-tists, engineering jurisprudence for the law of interest to engineers, archi-tectural jurisprudence for the law of interest to architects, are heard occa-sionally. These seem quite indefensible. But even if they were not to be criti-cized, they would not warrant Masonic jurisprudence, for the latter term calls to mind not that part of the general law of the land which has special interest for the Mason, but the internal law of the fraternity itself. We come back, therefore, to our question whether Masonic jurisprudence is simply a grandiose name for Masonic law or whether, on the other hand, there is a science of Masonic law distinct from the law of each Masonic jurisdiction? Is there, in other words, an organized body of knowledge above and behind each particular local Masonic law upon which the latter rests as fully and truly as the particular legal rules of one of our commonwealths rest upon the principles of general legal science and the principles of Anglo-Ameri-can legal tradition? For the moment I shall assume that there is, and my purpose in this course will be, not to expound dogmatically the rules of

Masonic law which obtain here or elsewhere, but to show, if I may, that there is a science of Masonic law, to examine its material and its methods, and to set forth its principles.

In studying the law of politically organized society we say that it may be expounded dogmatically, that is, the content and application of its several rules and principles may be investigated and set forth, or it may be studied by one of the methods of jurisprudence-- analytical, historical, or philosophical. In truth dogmatic study is of little value except as it makes use of and rests upon these methods of legal science. They justify themselves in the end by making for effective understanding and criticism and improvement of the law of each state. But they are methods of legal science generally, while the dogmatic method is applicable not to jurisprudence but to a particular body of law. We may study a particular body of law analytically, that is, we may investigate the structure, subject matter and rules of a legal system in order to reach by analysis the principles and theories which it logically presupposes, As a method of jurisprudence, however, the analytical method is comparative. It involves a comparative study of the purposes, methods and ideas common to developed systems of law by analysis of such systems and of their doctrines and institutions in their matured forms. Again, a particular body of law may be studied historically. That is, investigation may be made of the historical origin and development of the legal system and of its institutions and doctrines, looking to the past of the law to disclose the principles of the law of today. But here also, as a method of jurisprudence the historical method must be comparative. It involves a comparative study of the origin and development of law, of legal systems, and of particular doctrines and institutions in order to draw therefrom universal principles of legal science. Finally, a particular body of law may be studied philosophically. That is, investigation may be made of the philosophical bases of the institutions and doctrines of a legal system in order to reach its fundamental principles through philosophical speculation. When this method is pursued comparatively and the philosophical basis of law generally and of general legal institutions and universal legal doctrines is sought, in order to reach universal principles, the philosophical method becomes a method of jurisprudence. Formerly these three methods, the analytical, the historical and the philosophical, contended for the mastery. Today we recognize that no one of them is self-sufficient and that jurisprudence must employ each of them in order to achieve a well-rounded science.

If we apply these ideas to Masonic law, we may say that a dogmatic exposition of the law of any jurisdiction would, indeed, very likely be profitable. But it would be relatively of little value, certainly of little permanent value, unless it made use of and rested upon the analytical, the historical and the philosophical methods. Moreover these methods should be developed comparatively, as methods of a Masonic legal science, if they are to give their best results. On the other hand these methods are not pursued for their own sake. In the end they must justify themselves by making the law of each Masonic jurisdiction more scientific, better organized, more easy of comprehension and of application and more reflective for the purposes for which it exists. Unless he can give us principles of systematization, of criticism and of improvement in those parts of our law which are subject to change, the jurist has no claim upon the attention of a craft of workmen.

Another preliminary question confronts us. How far are we justified in speaking of Masonic law? Is the body of rules to which we give that name law in any proper sense of the term? Are we warranted in applying to it the methods and in attaching to it the ideas which are appropriate when treating of the law of politically organized society ?

There are three common uses of the term "law": (1) Law as used in the natural and physical sciences; (2) natural law or law of nature as the term has been used by writers on ethics, politics and the philosophy of law; (3) law in the juridical sense. In the sciences, law is used to mean deductions from human experience of the course of events. Thus the law of gravitation is a record of human observation and experience of the manner in which bodies which are free to move do in fact move toward one another. Similarly Grimm's law in philology is a record of the observations of philologists as to the manner in which consonantal changes have taken place in the several Aryan languages. By natural law ethical, philosophical and political writers mean the principles which philosophy and ethics discover as those which should govern human action and the adjustment of human relations, and hence as those with respect to which obligatory rules of human conduct ought to be framed. Law in the juridical sense is said to be the body of rules, principles and standards recognized or enforced by public or regular tribunals in the administration of justice. Obviously there is an idea in common here, namely, the idea of a rule or principle, underlying a sequence of events, whether natural or moral, or judicial. In this wide sense, therefore, we may speak of the rules or principles which underlay a sequence of events in a fraternal organization as law, just as we should so style the rules or principles underlying a sequence of events in a political society. But this wide use of the term law has been the subject of much objection and much dispute and we may put ourselves on firmer ground by looking at certain analogies between the rules which govern the decision of controversies and the adjustment of relations in a politically organized society and those which govern disputes and adjust relations in religious organizations and in fraternal organizations.

At bottom we must rest the whole structure of state and law upon the hard fundamental fact that in a finite world, human demands are infinite. If there were enough material goods to go around and enough room so that each of us might move in the widest orbit his fancy could picture or his desires could dictate without coming into collision with his fellow men, we should not need any elaborate system of balancing conflicting interests nor any elaborate machinery for putting into effect the standards for delimiting and enforcing interests which result from such balancing. Unhappily the material goods of existence do not suffice to give to each everything which he may claim or which he does claim. Hence to conserve the values of life and to eliminate waste men organize themselves and organize or invent rules and standards and principles by which to eliminate waste and make the available stock of values go as far as possible. In the beginning these organizations are simply groups of kindred. Presently religious and maternal organizations develop. Subsequently political organizations arise. In time trade and professional associations are added. All these seek in one way or another to secure to men values which might otherwise be dissipated. They have their justification in the necessity of conserving what would otherwise be lost in the struggle of individuals to satisfy infinite claims upon a limited store. Accordingly, if we look for a moment at the state, we see that it eliminates waste by means of the law in several ways. For one thing it furnishes a rule of decision in case of dispute and thus obviates resort to private war when controversies arise. One has only to consider what happens today in case of an industrial dispute in order to see what this means.

In an ordinary dispute between man and man today we have a measure of conduct which is ascertainable within reasonable limits in advance. If the dispute becomes acute, one party or the other may summon his adversary before a public tribunal and may have the dispute adjudicated upon the basis of settled rules, according to a settled procedure, and with reference to settled modes of redress. When the judgment is pronounced, it is not optional with the defeated party to adhere to it or not. The whole power of the state is behind it and the force of organized society may be invoked to carry it out. In an industrial dispute on the other hand, we have no clear measure of conduct. Each party is referred to his individual sense of fairness and to the general sense of fairness of the public at large. But in a highly diversified community in which groups and classes with apparently divergent interests understand each other none too well and have conflicting ideas of justice, general public opinion is seldom sufficiently definite and consistent to serve as a restraint upon the partisan notions of justice entertained by the contending parties and hence is left to be the judge of its own case. With no clear predetermined measure of adjustment of such controversies, with no settled mode of procedure, with no settled mode of redress and no strong, permanent tribunal, backed by the moral sense of the community, long tradition, and the force of the state, to pronounce and give effect to a judgment, there is no way to satisfy or to coerce the disputants and in practice, as like as not, the interests of each and the interests of society suffer equally. Society struggles to maintain its interest in the general security and to prevent waste under such circumstances by seeking peace at whatever sacrifice. It is not a question of equal and exact justice. The paramount demands of peace and good order are to be met first. The policy is not "let justice be done though the heavens fall," but "peace at any price." Hence society endeavors to put pressure upon the disputants, directly, indirectly, openly or covertly, to submit to arbitration and to abide the award. A public service company may be threatened with forfeiture of franchise. A private owner may be threatened with extra-legal sequestration of his property. Both parties may be threatened with a report as to the causes of the dispute and the issues involved to be made public after an official inquiry. Press, pulpit and platform may exhort and rebuke. Thus in one way or another a compromise or an arbitration may be brought about. But when such a result has been achieved, no guide has been provided for the next dispute. No precedent has resulted. Nothing has been accomplished beyond averting or terminating a condition of private war in that one case. The whole process is crude and wasteful. Every time that this happens we act over again the inception of law. The Roman magistrate who stepped between the contending litigants and called out, "Let go, both of you," the praetor who pronounced the interdict, "I forbid that violence take place," and the indirect devices whereby a case for arbitration was formulated, not upon direct statement of their claims by the parties but through indirectly inducing or coercing a reference or an arbitration, testify to a general condition of which the special condition that obtains in a modern industrial dispute is perhaps the last remnant. By furnishing a rule for decision and by furnishing a guide to conduct the law enables society to reconcile conflicting interests, to conserve values and to eliminate waste.

This same problem of reconciling conflicting interests, of conserving values and of eliminating waste arises in every group— in religious and fraternal organizations no less than in political organizations. And it is met in the same way. By slow and painful development of customs through experience, followed by deliberate formulation of rules invented for the purpose, men select out of the great mass of possible claims those which seem to call most urgently for security, define them, weigh them against other recognized interests and devise means for giving them effect. This process of recognizing, delimiting and securing interests when carried on by a political society is called lawmaking and the rules and standards of conduct and rules and principles of decision thereby set up are called law. In like manner the rules and standards of conduct and the rules and principles of decision developed or devised to secure interests and conserve values In the universal medieval church are called the canon law. No less justly may we apply to the rules and standards of conduct and the rules and principles of decision evolved or devised to secure interests and conserve values in our universal fraternal organization the name of Masonic law. For if it is said that we cannot enforce our law as the state enforces its law—that the sheriff and his posse looms in the background of the latter while the former is but hortatory—the answer must be that our law has behind it the same sanction that was behind the law of the medieval church, namely, excommunication and that this is essentially nothing else than the sanction of the earlier stages of the law of politically organized society — namely, outlawry. The group in each case casts out the individual who, through defiance of its law threatens a waste of the values which it seeks to secure.

Assuming, then, that we are justified in speaking of Masonic law, what are the component parts of our Masonic legal system; what are the jural materials with which the Masonic lawyer must work ? I venture to distinguish three types of rules: (1) The landmarks; (2) the Masonic common law; (3) Masonic legislation. I cannot deny that in so classifying the jural materials of Masonry I am influenced by our Anglo-American distinction of constitutional rules, common law and legislation. And one should not turn to such an analogy hastily or unadvisedly. For I shall endeavor to show in another connection that Masonic jurisprudence has suffered in this country from overzealous attempts to mould our law by the analogies of the political law of the time and place and from the hasty assumption that our American legal and political institutions might be relied upon to furnish principles of law for a universal fraternity. Nevertheless the craft has engaged the hearty service of great lawyers for at least two centuries and the revival from which we date the Masonry of today took place in a time and in a country in which certain legal and politic ideas were universally entertained and were almost taken to inhere in nature. Hence we have more than analogy — we have, if not a causal relation, at least a relation of great influence.

Presupposing this three-fold division, we have first, the landmarks, a small not clearly defined body of fundamentals which are beyond reach of change. They are the prescriptive or unwritten constitution (using constitution in the purely American sense) by which every thing must be judged ultimately and to which we must all conform. Second, we have Masonic common law — the body of tradition and doctrine, which falling short of the sanctity and authority of the landmarks, nevertheless is of such long standing, and so universal, and so well attested, that we should hesitate to depart from it and are perforce wont to rely upon it whether to apply our own law or to appreciate the law of our neighbors.

These first two elements of Masonic law rest in tradition and in doctrinal writing. They take the form of: (a) Tradition — the mode of conducting Masonic affairs which has been handed down from master to master, from lodge to lodge for centuries and embodies the experience of countless sincere, zealous, well-informed brothers; (b) treatises, of which Oliver's Institutes of Masonic Jurisprudence and Mackey's Masonic Jurisprudence are the best types; (c) decisions of Grand Masters and review thereof by Grand Lodges, recorded in the published proceedings of Grand Lodges, chiefly in America; and (d) reports of the committees on correspondence of our American Grand Lodges, in which the decisions in other jurisdictions are reviewed and criticized and a comparative and universal element is introduced which is of the highest value to the Masonic jurist. These committees on correspondence have been much kicked at and it cannot be denied that the work of some of them at times has been crude. Yet for the present purpose their work has been invaluable. No one who has studied Masonic jurisprudence attentively can fail to testify to the unifying force exerted by these committees. The stimulus of their criticism, even when ill directed has made our local Masonic jurists pause to think of the rest of the Masonic world; it has exerted the scientific influence which is always involved in comparison; it has worked everywhere for universality in our welter of independent local jurisdictions, each ambitious to make its own law.

The two main elements just enumerated make up the unwritten law of Masonry. A third element, namely, Grand Lodge legislation, of which our American Grand Lodges have been exceedingly prolific, constitutes the written law of Masonry.

A moment's digression is required to explain these terms. As soon as legal systems attain any degree of maturity, they are made up of two elements: A traditional element and an imperative element. Following the Roman jurists, the traditional element is generally known in jurisprudence by the name of the unwritten law — jus non scriptum — and the imperative element by the name of the written law — jus scriptum; not that we do not find the principles and rules of each today only in writings, but because the latter was deliberately and authoritatively reduced to writing at its inception.

Our main interest is in the unwritten law — the traditional element — which, except as local decisions interpret or apply local legislation, proceeds or purports to proceed on universal lines and is or seeks to be in principle permanent and general, even as legislation is ephemeral and local.

Let me develop this point a bit. As has been said, a developed legal system is made up of two elements, a traditional element and an enacted or imperative element. Although at present the balance in our law is shifting gradually to the side of the enacted element, the traditional element is still by far the more important. In the first instance, we must rely upon it to meet all new problems, for the legislator acts only after they attract attention. But even after the legislator has acted, it is seldom if ever that his foresight extends to all the details of his problem or that he is able to do more than provide a broad, if not a crude outline. Hence even in the field of the enacted law, the traditional element of the legal system plays a chief part. We must rely upon it to fill the gaps in legislation, to develop the principles introduced by legislation and to interpret them. Let us not forget that so-called interpretation is not merely ascertainment of the legislative intent. If it were, it would be the easiest instead of the most difficult of judicial tasks. Where the legislator has had an intent and has sought to express it, there is seldom a question of interpretation. The difficulties arise in the myriad cases with respect to which the law maker had no intention because he had never thought of them — indeed perhaps he could never have thought of them.

Here under the guise of interpretation the court, willing or unwilling, must to some extent make the law, and our security that it will be made as law and not as arbitrary rule lies in the judicial and juristic tradition from which the materials of judicial law-making are derived. Accordingly the traditional element of the legal system is and must be used even in an age of copious legislation, to supplement, round out and develop the enacted element, and in the end it usually swallows up the latter and incorporates its results in the body of tradition. Moreover a large field is always unappropriated by enactment, and here the traditional element is supreme. In this part of the law fundamental ideas change slowly. The alterations wrought here and there by legislation, not always consistent with one another, do not produce a general advance. Indeed they may be held back at times in the interests, real or supposed, of uniformity and consistency, through the influence of the traditional element. It is obvious, therefore, that above all else the condition of the law depends upon the condition of this element of the legal system.

Another feature of the twofold composition of developed legal systems is of no less importance. The traditional element rests at first upon the traditional mode of advising litigants on the part of those upon whom tribunals rely for guidance or upon the usage and practice of tribunals. Later it rests upon juristic science and the habitual modes of thought of a learned profession. Thus the ultimate basis of its authority is reason and conformity to ideals of right. On the other hand the imperative element rests upon enactment. It rests upon the expressed will of the sovereign. The basis of its authority is the power of the state.

The parallel with Masonic law is exact. With us, the most important of our jural materials are in the traditional element.

First, we must rely upon the traditional element to meet all new problems, and the normal course of growth in Masonic law is: (1) A new application of a traditional principle by the decision of a Grand Master; (2) review thereof in a Grand Lodge; (3) comment thereon by the various committees on correspondence; (4) the growth of a consensus of opinion on the subject among Masonic jurists; and (5) incorporation in some text book of Masonic law or in declaratory legislation. Secondly, we must rely on the traditional element to fill all gaps in Masonic legislation. Thirdly, we must rely on it to interpret legislation and to develop legislation. Fourthly, above all, as we are a universal institution and ought to legislate cautiously, we must rely on the traditional element to furnish the principles of legislation and a critique of legislation.

Accordingly it is of the first importance to have a theory of the unwritten law of Masonry and an organized, systematic science of this traditional element of our law — in other words, to have a science of Masonic jurisprudence.

What are the data of this science ? What are the materials which we may use in constructing it?

I take it they are five: (1) History; (2) general Masonic tradition; (3) philosophy; (4) logical (or systematic) construction on the basis of history, philosophy and tradition; and (5) authentic modern materials of Masonic common law.

Let me take these up in order. First as to history. Here there are two questions: (a) What materials does Masonic history furnish which are important for Masonic jurisprudence; (b) what is the function of history in Masonic jurisprudence how and for what purpose should we use history in this connection ? On such an occasion one can only speak summarily. In a few words, the historical materials which are important for the Masonic jurist seem to be five:

(1) The manuscript constitutions of British Freemasons — a series of manuscripts the oldest of which go back to the fourteenth century, which are the foundation of authentic Masonic history. These are of especial importance on the subject of the landmarks. Thus, when we trace in the manuscripts the old charge to be true to God and holy church and the new charge of 1738 that if the Mason understands his art aright he will never be a stupid atheist, history reinforces the tradition contained in the master's obligation.

(2) Seventeenth and eighteenth-century notices of English Masonry prior to 1717. From these materials we are able to see how Masons met and what they meant by a lodge prior to the rise of Grand-Lodge Masonry and are enabled to distinguish between the landmarks and the common law as to Masonic organization.

(3) Old lodge records in England and Scotland. These also throw great light upon the organization of the Craft prior to 1717. When we find presidents and wardens and deacons as the highest officers of lodges, we see again what was from the beginning and what is simply common law.

(4) Eighteenth-century writers who had or purported to have access to traditions current among Masons at and prior to the organization of the Grand Lodge of England in 1717 and to old manuscripts not now extant. Even if some or much of the information which they purport to give on the basis of such traditions and such manuscripts is apocryphal, it has entered into the stream of subsequent Masonic tradition and may not be overlooked.

(5) Grand Lodge records, beginning in England in 1723, which show the settled practice of the formative period of Masonry as we know it today.

Of these five classes of historical materials, the fourth calls for some special notice. It is made up of three well-known books which have exerted an almost controlling influence upon our ideas of Masonic history and have largely determined Masonic tradition. These books are: Anderson's *Constitution* (1723, second edition 1738), Preston's *Illustrations* (1772) and Dermott's *Ahiman Rezon* (1756, second edition 1764). It would be out of place to attempt an appraisal of their historical value here. Moreover the thorough-going critique of Gould, which has definitely overthrown much which had long been accepted on the authority of these books has not wholly destroyed their importance for Masonic jurisprudence. As Hobbes puts it, "authority not truth makes the law." It may well happen that historical mistakes may become fixed in the legal fabric. For example, Lord Coke very likely erred in much that he laid down in his Second Institute as to the history of our Anglo-American constitutional doctrine of the supremacy of law. Yet his writing is the foundation of our public law and his results have amply justified themselves. It is no fatal objection in practical affairs that the conclusions must sustain the premises. Hence if Anderson and Preston and Dermott cannot be vouched for landmarks, they must be read diligently in order to reach the sources of much of our Masonic common law.

Let us turn now to the other question, what are the uses of Masonic history ? One use is to correct tradition, as for example, in the case of the apocryphal long list of royal and noble Grand Masters. Another is to hold philosophy in bounds, as for example, in the case of the controversy which raged once in one of our American Grand Lodges as to the wearing of white gloves, on the theory that gloves were unknown at the time of the building of the temple, or, again, in the rejection of the letter G on philosophical grounds by another of our Grand Lodges. Another use is to test doctrinal (systematic, logical) exposition, as in the case of Mackey's twenty-five landmarks. But this correction by history should not be pressed too far. It should not be used as the basis of rejecting settled Masonic common law, shown by universal practice since the end of the eighteenth century. For example, nothing is better settled than the doctrines of territorial jurisdiction in Craft Masonry and the impropriety of invasion of jurisdiction. If there are no landmarks here, there are settled principles of Masonic conflict of laws which are a part of the universal law of the Craft.

Our second main source of law is tradition. Today this is set forth in the form of doctrinal exposition and Grand-Lodge decision. Much of it is declared by Grand-Lodge legislation. It is of the highest value in fixing the principles of Masonic common law. But elsewhere it is dangerous. It must always be corrected by careful historical consideration of whether the tradition in question is authentic, immemorial and pure.

Our third main source of law is philosophy, that is, deduction from principles found by philosophical study of the ends and purpose of Masonry — for example, deduction from the principle of universality, from the principle of organization of moral sentiments of mankind, from the principle of furthering human civilization. It may be compared with the metaphysical method in jurisprudence which seeks to deduce all legal rules from or correct them by a fundamental principle of human freedom. Philosophy is chiefly useful as a check on Masonic history. For example, if one were to look only to history, he might make a strong argument that the dinner or banquet following the work on important occasions was a landmark. Certainly as far back as we have accounts of Masonic work we find the brethren sitting about the board in this way. But consideration of the purposes and ends of the order shows us at once that we have here but an incident of ordinary human social intercourse. So in the case of the objection to white gloves above referred to. The Masonic philosopher perceives at once that we have here a traditional symbol and that purely historical considerations cannot be suffered to prevail.

Our fourth main source of law is logical construction. It has the same place with us as juristic science has in the law of the state. It is of the first importance if the data are sound and are well used. Mackey's famous text book of Masonic jurisprudence (1859) is still the best example of the use of logical construction.

The fifth main source of Masonic law is to be found in authentic modern materials of Masonic customary law and in settled Masonic usage since the last half of the eighteenth century. Indeed the general principles of this settled usage have all but the force of landmarks. Thus Mackey recognizes: (1) Landmarks; (2) general laws or regulations; (3) local laws or regulations. Here the second is substantially what I call Masonic common law and the third what I call Masonic legislation. Mackey says of the second: "These are all those regulations that have been enacted by such bodies as had at the time universal jurisdiction. They operate, therefore, over the Craft whereso-ever dispersed; and as the paramount bodies which enacted them have long ceased to exist, it would seem that they are unrepealable. It is generally agreed that these general or universal laws are to be found in the old constitutions or charges, so far as they were recognized and accepted by the Grand Lodge of England at the revival in 1717 and adopted previous to the year 1726." This would receive Anderson's first edition without question as a conclusive exposition of the principles of the traditional element. Today it is clear that we cannot accept it. But the idea at the bottom of Mackey's system is sound.

I take it we must distinguish two things. (a) We may perceive certain settled principles adhered to by all regular and well-governed lodges since the last quarter of the eighteenth century. For example, with one exception it has always been recognized that at least three lodges are required to set up a Grand Lodge. But we must be cautious here. It will be noticed that Mackey assumes that fluidity is at an end by 1721. We cannot accept this proposition. We must recognize a great deal of fluidity till much later. But Masonry is not bound to retain forever the fluidity of the first half of the eighteenth century. (b) Next we must differentiate from the principles themselves the development of these principles (i) by logical deduction and juristic speculation, and (ii) by judicial empiricism in the decisions of Grand Masters and the review thereof by Grand Lodges.

The latter is almost wholly American and much of it is worthy to rank with the best achievements of legal development in any political organization. If the law of the medieval church became for a time the law of the world and gave ideas and doctrines to the law of the state which are valuable for all time, it is not at all impossible that our universal organization, coming much later to the work of law-making, may in its turn develop legal ideas of universal value and thus contribute indirectly to the furtherance of civilization while contributing directly thereto in its ordinary work.

FREEMASONS IN THE AMERICAN REVOLUTION
by Charles S. Lobingier

Brother J.E. Morcombe in a series of scholarly papers once declared (1) that after "a very serious course of historical reading extending through several months and covering the period of the last three centuries" he was regretfully forced" to reject "as mainly mythical the alleged participation of American Masonic Lodges, as such, in affairs of the Revolution."

A statement like this, coming from such a diligent and distinguished Masonic student, deserves consideration and analysis. If correct it destroys many cherished beliefs; if incorrect it ought, in justice to the craft, past and present, to be so declared.

My own investigations have led me to a somewhat different conclusion. And while I am not prepared to say that the direct "participation of American Lodges" in our struggle for nationality was extensive, still I cannot but feel that their indirect assistance was great and their actual participation at certain stages determining. I will, therefore, state the results of my survey (2) of this field in language employed when it was first completed and, that my readers may themselves be enabled to judge of the soundness of my conclusions, I will, for each important statement, cite my authority.

At the outbreak of the Revolution Masonic lodges in America were few and feeble. The oldest of them had existed less than half a century (3) and the membership was exceedingly small (4). But what was lacking in members was more than supplied in quality. The Freemasons of that period included the flower of colonial citizenship and their very fewness was a source of strength. In a small lodge all could know and trust each other; all felt the need of absolute secrecy in deliberation — of solidarity in action. Hence it is not strange that some of these colonial lodges became the centers of revolutionary propaganda (5).

ST. ANDREW'S LODGE

Foremost among these was the Lodge of St. Andrew at Boston. Founded in 1756 and chartered by the Grand Lodge of Scotland in 1760, it began its career independent of English influence and just in time to share in the opening scenes of the war for independence. Joseph Warren was its Master, Paul Revere one of its early initiates and secretaries and later its Master, and on its rolls were the names of John Hancock, and James Otis and many others who are now recognized as the leading characters of that eventful epoch.

And almost every important movement in the patriotic cause in Boston, preceding and precipitating the Revolution, may be traced back directly or indirectly to St. Andrew's Lodge.

The famous "Sons of Liberty," organized in 1765 to resist the enforcement of the Stamp Act, were but an offshoot of this Lodge, and was also the "North End Caucus" (6) to which was committed the execution of some of the most daring plans of the patriots. Both of these organizations met at the Green Dragon Tavern which was owned and occupied by St. Andrew's Lodge, and the members of the latter were leaders in the former. It was at this tavern that the historic Boston Tea Party was planned by Warren, Revere and other members of St. Andrew's (7). The records of the lodge disclose that on the evening after the tea-laden ships arrived in Boston Harbor there was an adjournment on account of small attendance and the secretary adds the significant note that "consignees of tea took the brethren's time." The minutes of December 16, 1773, the date of the tea party, show that the lodge was again adjourned until the next evening (8). Its members were among that band of enthusiasts who had boarded the ships and were rapidly heaving the obnoxious tea into the waters of Boston Harbor.

In the days which followed it was Paul Revere of St. Andrew's Lodge who earned the title of "The Patriotic Mercury" or "The Messenger of the Revolution." Thousands of miles he rode on horseback, spreading the news of the destruction of the tea, bearing despatches to other colonies, to New York and Philadelphia, to Provincial and Continental Congresses (9). And on that memorable night before the battle of Lexington it was by order of the Master of St. Andrew's, Joseph Warren, that Bro. Paul Revere set out upon his famous ride to Concord to warn his countrymen of the foe's approach — a ride which has been immortalized by the magic pen of Longfellow who tells us that,

"Through all our history to the last In the hour of darkness and peril and need The people will waken and listen to hear The hurrying hoofbeats of that steed And the midnight message of Paul Revere."

And when at last the storm, which for years had been gathering, burst in all its fury, it was St. Andrew's Lodge which furnished the first great martyr to American liberty. Joseph Warren, Major General in the Continental Army, fell at Bunker Hill; and thus the lodge which had almost initiated the war gave up its Master in the battle which determined forever the supremacy of the American arms in Massachusetts. No other organization, civic or military, of its numbers, can be compared to St. Andrew's Lodge in the extent of its contributions to the American cause. The title "Cradle of Liberty," which has been applied to Faneuil Hall, rightfully belongs to the Green Dragon Tavern where gathered that little band of Masons who precipitated the American Revolution.

THE OTHER PATRIOTIC LODGES

But there were other lodges which rendered valuable services in the war for independence. St. John's Provincial Grand Lodge at Boston, the older rival of St. Andrew's, furnished, in the person of its Deputy Grand Master Ridley, the engineer who planned the American fortifications at Bunker Hill (10). St. George's Lodge at Schnectady, N. Y., where many Revolutionary officers were made Masons, honored itself and the order by appropriating lodge funds for the support of the families of its members who had been taken prisoners (11).

The intimate connection between Masonry and the patriotic movements is also shown by the growth of the order at this time. Master's Lodge alone, at Albany, received eighty-three new members during the historic year 1776 (12).

MILITARY LODGES

But the most important service, after the Revolution was fairly launched, was rendered by the lodges formed in the Continental Army. There were ten of these (13), they were scattered among the camps from Massachusetts to North Carolina, and their growth was fostered and encouraged by the Commander-in-Chief. Washington himself attended their communications frequently — now as a visitor, meeting soldier brethren on the level (14) and now as Master sitting in the Oriental chair and bringing a candidate to Masonic light (15). It was in one of these lodges — American Union at Morristown, N. J. — that Lafayette is believed to have received his degrees (16). Lodge meetings were sometimes held in officers' tents (17) and sometimes, as in the case of the army encamped on the Hudson, in a permanent building specially erected for that purpose (18). And so active were these military Masons that a movement was started and several conventions held at Morristown with a view of establishing an American General Grand Lodge and making Washington Grand Master of the United States. (19).

It is difficult to overestimate the strategic value of these army lodges. In the first place they promoted fellowship and solidarity in the ranks and sympathy between officers and men. In an army where the humblest private might sit in lodge on a level with the Commander-in-Chief there arose a spirit of self-sacrifice, mutual helpfulness and devotion — an esprit du corps — which no hireling soldiery could have. Where the distinctions or rank were lost in the ties of brotherhood, even the sufferings of that terrible winter at Valley Forge might be made endurable.

Again, the prevalence of Masonry in the patriotic army insured secrecy in the plans of campaign and fidelity in their execution. Councils of war it is said, were frequently held in the lodge room where their deliberations were under the double seal of Masonry and patriotism. Generals could entrust their dispatches to couriers who were brother Masons and feel certain that nothing would be divulged. Thus our eighteenth century brethren formed the strong arm of the Continental service. It is claimed that nearly every American general was a Mason (20); certainly the leading ones were. Even the allies, Lafayette, the Frenchman, and Steuben (21) and Dekalb, the Germans, were members of the order. John Paul Jones, the founder of our navy, is known to have petitioned St. Bernard's Lodge at Kirkcudbright, Scotland, and probably was a member of it (22). Had the Freemasons been withdrawn from the Continental forces the Revolution must have been a dismal failure.

OUR BRETHREN OF THE OPPOSING FORCES

But we must never forget that not all Freemasons of the Revolution were enrolled in the patriotic ranks— that they were numerous in the opposing army as well. Peter Ross, the historian of the Grand Lodge of New York, records as operating during the war in that state more than thirty British military lodges (22a). And to the fact that Masons were actively engaged on both sides is due some of the most gratifying incidents of the war. It has been said that the fairest flowers are those that bloom over the wall of party; but how much more must be said of those that bloom amid the strife of armies.

Early in the war an event occurred that proved the strength of the Masonic tie. At the battle of the Cedars near Montreal, Col. John McKinstry, a Freemason, was captured by a band of Indians, allies of the British, whose chief was the celebrated Joseph Brand, also a Mason. In accordance with savage custom the prisoner was bound to a stake, fagots were piled around him, and the torch was about to be applied, when he gave to Chief Brand the sign which Masons know the world around—the grand hailing sign of distress. Indian though he was, the chief recognized the sign and ordered the torture to cease, and he and his captive became fast friends for the rest of their lives (23).

Again, in 1779, Joseph Burnam, a Mason who was held by the British as a prisoner of war in New York City, escaped and sought shelter in the Green Bay Tree Tavern, kept by another Mason named Hopkins. This tavern served as a meeting place for St. John's Lodge, which was composed mostly of British officers. The fugitive was secreted in the tavern garret which was just above the lodge room, and while he was reclining at night on the planks which formed the garret floor these gave way and precipitated the unfortunate guest into the center of the lodge in the very midst of its deliberations. The landlord, who was also the Tiler, was called upon for an explanation, and he, like a good Mason, made a clean breast of the whole affair. Whereupon the members of the lodge took up a contribution for the fugitive brother and, though his enemy in war, assisted him to reach the American lines across the Hudson River (24).

Another instance of Masonic magnanimity occurred when the brave Baron DeKalb, our German ally, was slain at the battle of Camden in 1780. Although he had crossed the Atlantic to take part in a quarrel that was not his, against the British, he was buried by them with both Masonic and military honors (25).

But perhaps the most significant illustration of the effect of Masonry on the war was the action taken by the Grand Lodge of Scotland. It is well known that the war was unpopular in many parts of Great Britain; but some of the subordinate Scottish Lodges, urged perhaps by government officials, had offered bounties for recruits to the army. When the Grand Lodge met it condemned this practice in unmistakable terms and in its instructions declared: "Masonry is an order of peace and it looks on all mankind to be at peace or at war with each other as subjects of contending countries." (26)

RECIPROCITY IN THE AMERICAN ARMY

These are illustrations which, thanks to Masonic teaching, reveal the foe in a better light than some are wont to think of him. Let us notice some expressions of the same spirit on the American side.

At the battle of Princeton, 1776, Captain William Leslie, a Mason and son of the Earl of Leven, of the British Army, received a severe wound. He was taken in charge by Dr. Benjamin Rush, the celebrated surgeon who was then on Gen. Washington's staff, but was found to be "past all surgery." He was also buried with Masonic and military honors and this fact was announced by Col. Fitzgerald, Gen. Washington's aide, who entered the British Camp for that purpose under a flag of truce. Later Dr. Rush erected a monument, which may still be seen, at Brothel Leslie's grave "as a mark of esteem for his worth and respect for his noble family (27)."

Lodge Unity was a military lodge in the 17th foot of the British army. In 1779, while the regiment was engaged in a skirmish, the constitution and jewels of the lodge were lost, but were returned to it by Col. Parsons of the American Union Lodge in the opposing army, with a letter reciting that,

"As Masons we are disarmed of that resentment which stimulates to undistinguished desolation; and however our political sentiments may impel us in the public dispute, we are still brethren, and (our professional duty apart) ought to promote the happiness and advance the weal of each other." (25)

An even more striking instance occurred when the Masonic chest of the 46th British infantry was captured by the Americans. Upon hearing of it, Gen. Washington ordered the chest and other articles of value returned to the owners accompanied by a guard of honor (29). *The London Freemason's*

Magazine, commenting on the circumstances, from an English standpoint, says:

"The surprise, the feelings of both officers and men may be imagined when they perceived the flag of truce that announced this elegant compliment from their noble opponent but still more noble brother. The guard of honor, their flutes playing a sacred march, the chest containing the constitution and implements of the craft borne aloft like another Ark of the Covenant, equally by Englishmen and Americans, who, lately engaged in the strife of war, now marched through the enfiladed ranks of the gallant regiment, that, with presented arms and colors, hailed the glorious act by cheers which the sentiment rendered sacred as the hallelujahs of an angel's song."

Thus, above the storm and stress of armed strife, the soothing spirit of Masonic fellowship brooded like a bird of calm. If Masons precipitated and promoted the struggle they likewise mitigated its horrors and made possible the disclosure of the noblest traits in both American and Briton. It is the proudest heritage of Revolutionary Masons on both sides that the fraternal tie was one which not even the shock of arms could sever, and that amid the fiercest passions engendered by war they never quite forgot they were brethren. The record of this forms the fairest, brightest page in the history of the Revolution.

IN THE COUNCILS OF STATE

When we turn from scenes of carnage to the more peaceful haunts of diplomat and statesman, during the Revolution, we find Freemasons there active and influential. It is a notable fact that the earliest suggestion of a Federal Union of the American colonies came from the first American Grand Master, Daniel Coxe, who in 1730 received a deputation as Provincial Grand Master, made this suggestion in a work published as early as 1716, (30) and may therefore properly be called the first Federalist. It was this idea, adopted later and advocated by another eminent Mason and Provincial Grand Master, Benjamin Franklin, that grew into the union established by the constitution framed two generations later. The Declaration of Independence, it has been declared, (31) was the work of a Mason and many of the signers of that instrument are believed to have been members of our order (32). Freemasons were foremost in the Philadelphia Convention that framed the Federal Constitution and thus completed the work of the war. Besides Washington, the President, and Franklin, the Nestor, of that body, Hamilton, the genius of the Convention, was a Mason (33).

AT THE COURTS OF EUROPE

But after all it may be that Masonry's most effective service to the American cause was rendered not at home but abroad. We know that the aid of France was a powerful, if not indispensable factor in the outcome of the war and that the sympathy of other Continental powers was advantageous. But why should these haughty monarchists of Europe look with favor upon the struggling republic of the New World ? Why did they not turn the same deaf ear as recently to the Boer envoys? There seems to have been some mysterious influence which changed their once hostile attitude into one of friendship; and recent investigations have led to the belief that this influence was the Masonic order (34).

When Franklin, the Freemason, went to Paris to plead the American cause at the court of St. Germain, he naturally sought out the members of the fraternity. At the "Lodge of the Nine Muses," where he often attended, he met the intellect and statesmanship of the gay French capital, and it is believed that partly, at least, through these influences he was enabled to reach the ear of Louis XVI, to secure for us the French fleet and army, and thus to turn the tide of the war in favor of the American cause at its darkest hour. And thus the record of Masonic service in the Revolution is complete. There was no part of it in which Masons did not share and no important phase which would probably have succeeded but for them.

But we fail to grasp the full significance of this noble record if we see in it only a source of pride and gratification. It is all this but much more; for every page imposes duty, obligation, responsibility. If it be true, as the record seems to teach, that American nationality was largely brought about by Masons, and that to this end the best energies of the craft were devoted in the trying times of the Revolution; if our predecessors gave "their lives, their fortunes and their sacred honor" to start the republic on its glorious career, surely we can best prove true to the traditions of American Masonry by continuing the work which they began. Our advantages, if not our opportunities, are greater than theirs. The feeble fraternity of that day has become a powerful order now — from a few thousands it has grown to nearly two millions, carefully selected from the ranks of American citizenship. Its representatives are found in every official station (35) from Presidents (36) down. What possibilities for good government and high political ideals do these facts express; what a mighty leverage for civic progress and reform ! And this is the highest lesson taught us as a craft by Freemasons of the American Revolution: To place patriotism above partisanship, to preserve and extend the free institutions of the republic, to maintain the honor and dignity of the nation at home and abroad, and thus to realize the lofty ideals of our eighteenth century brethren, bequeathing them as a priceless heritage to generations yet unborn.

REFERENCES:

(1) Record of Intolerance, 21 Am. Tyler-Keystone 549. See a reply in Vol. 22 of the same periodical, page 113.

(2) Undertaken while preparing an address as Grand Orator before the Grand Lodge of Nebraska.

(3) The earliest American Lodge is claimed to have been St. John's at Philadelphia, formed about 1730. See Gould, *History of Freemasonry*, Vol. IV, p. 233, et seq.

(4) Bro. Ross, historian of the Grand Lodge, concludes (N. Y. Grand Lodge Proc. 1900) that there were not more than 250 members of New York Lodges during the Revolution.

(5) There seems every reason to admit what has been so often claimed by our historians, that the Masonic Lodges scattered throughout the country were as beacon lights of liberty, and that within our tiled doors the Revolution was fostered and strengthened." — Ross, Historian of Grand Lodge, N. Y. Proceedings (1900), p. 315.

(6) Goss, *Life of Paul Revere*, (1891), pp. 117, 121-2.

(7) Centennial Memorial of the Lodge of St. Andrew, and the Massachusetts Grand Lodge (1870).

(8) Goss, Life of Paul Revere, (1891), pp. 121-2; Gould, *History of Freemasonry*, Vol. IV, p. 347.

(9) Id. p. 118 et seq.

(10) Gould, *History of Freemasonry*, Vol. IV, p. 220.

(11) Ross, Historian of Grand Lodge, N. Y. Proceedings (1900) p. 313.

(12) Id. p. 315.

(13) Gould, *History of Freemasonry*, Vol. IV, pp. 222, 227.

(14) Ross, Historian of Grand Lodge, N. Y. Proc. (1900) pp. 298, 305; Hayden, *Washington and His Masonic Compeers; Capt. G. P. Brown* in *American Tyler*, Dec. 15, 1900; Mackey, *Encyclopedia of Freemasonry*, p. 869.

(15) Ross, Historian of Grand Lodge, N. Y. Proc. (1900) p. 308.

(16) Gould, History of Freemasonry, Vol. IV, p. 224.

(17) Id.; Ross, Historian Grand Lodge, N. Y. Proc. (1900) p. 308.

(18) Capt. G. P. Brown in American Tyler. Dec. 15, 1900, says: "American Union Lodge was the banner lodge of the Continental Army. It had a very large membership, including several of Washington's foremost generals. In 1782, while the patriot host was encamped on the banks of the Hudson the attendance of that renowned lodge became so large that it was necessary to erect a building for its regular meetings. At a stated assembly of the lodge the question arose. General Washington was among the large number of visitors present and spoke at some length on the erection of a suitable building for Masonic purposes. And it was but a few days later when the

noble-hearted commander-in-chief and eminent Freemason ordered the erection of a wooden structure. It was nearly sixty feet long and of the old style, one-story plan. It formed a complete oblong square. It had but one door, which was on the west end; its windows were fairly good size, square and over six feet from the ground, thus to keep off the cowan and eavesdropper which were so plenty in the Continental army at that time. ... One of the many noted Masonic celebrations held within those sacred walls was the festival of Saint John the Baptist, June 24, A. L. 5782."

(19) Gould, Vol. IV, pp. 224-5; Ross, pp. 304-5; Mackey, *Encyclopedia of Freemasonry*, p. 870.

(20) Gould, Vol. IV, p. 224. G. P. Brown, in the article last above quoted, gives the following list of those who participated in the celebrations there mentioned: "Generals Washington, Gist, Putnam, Hamilton, Jackson, Armstrong, Parsons, Heath, Thompson, Patterson, Clinton, Dayton, Greaton, Brooks, Huntington; Colonels Cilley, Gridley, Burbeck, Nixon, Bradford, Clarke, Parke, Gray, Johnston, Sherman; Captains Marshall, Brown, Hait, Coit, Redfield, Lacey, Chapman, Ten Eyck; Lieutenants Heart, Hosmor, Hobart, Buxton, Russell, Barker, Sherman, Curtis, Heath, Bush, Spear, Cleveland, Palmer and a host of petty officers and privates. General John Stark, the hero of Bennington, was a Mason, initiated, according to Brown, in St. John's Lodge, No. 1, Portsmouth, N. H.; according to Ross, in Master's Lodge, Albany, N. Y.

(21) Baron Steuben was a member of Trinity and an honorary member of Holland Lodge, both of New York. See N. Y. Grand Lodge Proc. (1900), p. 309.

(22) See *American Tyler*, Vol. 15, p. 478

(22a) See also Sachse, *Old Masonic Lodges of Pennsylvania*, 1730-1800, especially the chapter on Unity Lodge No. 18, A. Y. M., abstracted in the New Age, XXIV, 539.

(23) Stone, Life of Brant, (1838), Vol. I, pp. 18-33; Vol. II, p. 156; Gould, *History of Freemasonry*, Vol. IV, p. 221; Ross, N.Y. Grand Lodge Proc. (1900), 307.

(24) Ross, N. Y. Grand Lodge Proc. (1900), 302, giving an extract from the printed history of St. John's Lodge; Mitchell, *History of Freemasonry* (1817), p. 501.

(25) Gould, *History of Freemasonry*, Vol. IV, p. 222.

(26) Lyon, *History of the Lodge of Edinburgh*, p. 83; Mackey, *Encyclopedia of Freemasonry*, p. 868.

(27) Sachse, *Old Masonic Lodges of Pennsylvania*, abstracted in New Age, XXIV, 539.

(28) Ross, 2, 98, 99. The letter is reprinted in the New Age (XXIV, 639), from Sachse, *Old Masonic Lodges of Pennsylvania*. This Lodge Unity appears to have received successive warrants from the Grand Lodges of Ireland, Scotland and Pennsylvania.

(29) Ross, 299, 300.

(30) The work was entitled *A Description of the English Province of Carolina.* See Gould, *History of Freemasonry,* Vol. IV, pp. 231-2; Ross, N. Y. Grand Lodge Proc. (1900), pp. 295-6.

(31) Capt. G. P. Brown, of Boston, in a private letter, furnished the information on which this statement is based

(32) P.G.M. Baird in THE BUILDER (II, 351), mentions twenty-three. Cf. Gould, *History of Freemasonry,* Vol. IV, p. 220; N. Y. Grand Lodge Proc. (1900) p. 81; John Carson Smith in American Tyler-Keystone, XXIII, 300.

(33) Ross, N. Y. Grand Lodge Proc. (1900), 305

(34) The late Gen. John Carson Smith, of Illinois, to whom I am indebted for favors, conducted these investigations.

(35) In a recent enumeration of the Massachusetts and New Hampshire Legislatures more than one-third of the members were found to be Masons; in one branch the proportion was one-half. 15 Annals of American Academy 81.

(36) P.G.M. Baird in THE BUILDER (II, 351), presents a list of seventeen Presidents who were Masons, and mentions another (Grant) who may have taken the E. A. degree. This is more than two-thirds of the whole number.

A BIRD'S-EYE VIEW OF MASONIC HISTORY
by H.L. Haywood

This essay was written at the request of the Committee on Masonic Research of the Grand Lodge of Iowa and is being published in pamphlet form by that Committee under the title "A Vest Pocket History of Freemasonry." It is intended to be given by lodges to newly-raised candidates. Prepared for such purpose, it does not attempt to be inclusive, though it is more than a mere introduction to the subject. The author makes no claim to authoritativeness or to finality, yet the view-point of the whole is supported by the most notable of modern writers. The rich and varied story of Freemasonry in America is barely mentioned and other equally important chapters of the great History of Freemasonry have been entirely omitted. The Research Committee has announced that other pamphlets intended to cover omitted subjects with equal simplicity and informality will follow.

Modern scientists have given us a new method for studying the past. We do not interpret the history of the Greeks, the Romans, the Hebrews, or any other ancient people, as once we did. All the records have been newly judged. We may be thankful that the records of Freemasonry have been likewise critically examined because we have gained thereby a clearer account of the beginnings of the Order. The books left us by the earlier Masonic writers are usually admirable in spirit and purpose but their historical portions must be received with caution: historians, archaeologists, philologists, and other scientists have given us so many new facts and have disproved so many time-honored traditions, that we must learn to read Masonic history with a new mind. In this brief and simple account of the matter the writer has attempted to follow these scholars as closely as possible.

But this does not mean that the present, or any other modern account of our history, is to be accepted as final. Far from it. It is too early to write such a history. In spite of all our discoveries much fog still hangs over our beginnings. The records since the organization of the first Grand Lodge in 1717 are usually reliable and fairly complete, but for the history prior to that date such facts as we have are mixed up with a vast deal of myth and guesswork. One must feel his way through the dark, and it is therefore better to remain content with the facts, few as they are, than to yield to the influence of any one of the - numerous fantastic theories which trace Freemasonry back to every nook and corner of ancient times; back to Noah's ark, for example, or to the creation of the world. In the present essay, modest as is its scope, an attempt will be made to indicate what we may safely believe concerning our ancestry; but even so this account is not in any sense offered as the last word on the subject.

Also it is wise to leave alone those enthusiastically held theories, which are usually as vain as they are numerous, that trace our Fraternity's beginnings to magic, or to some other form of occultism. Most of us are content to achieve results by familiar and natural methods; but there have always been men who have believed that back of the normal forces of Nature there are hidden mysterious forces which are known only to a few of the initiated, and they have tried to use these "forces" as a short cut to power. Instead of digging gold out of the ground as sensible men do, they have tried to create it by the transmutation of iron, or copper, or tin; instead of building up health of the body by the means known to all of us: simple living, rest, exercise, and the like, they have sought the Elixir of Life; instead of learning wisdom as all of us men are obliged to learn it they have hunted around for the Philosopher's Stone. There have been many societies in existence in the past for the purpose of teaching to initiates the so-called "secrets" of this kind of thing, and these societies are called "Occult Fraternities" because what they have practised is "occultism." There were many such fraternities in ancient times and in the Middle Ages, and some of them possessed a certain amount of wisdom and true lore; some of them, no doubt, contributed something to the evolution of Freemasonry; but it is all wrong to suppose, as some do, that Freemasonry was created by these occultists or that Freemasonry itself is a form of occultism. It is nothing of the kind, for it has grown out of, and is built upon, the same normal experiences of everyday life.

In Egyptian mythology there is a story singularly like our legend of Hiram Abif. Confucius spoke of a "square and compass man," and Mencius, another great Chinese teacher, sometimes talked like a Mason. There is much said in Hebrew tradition about builders. Amid the Pompeiian ruins was found a pedestal on which were engraved certain familiar symbols. In Peruvian architecture archaeologists have discovered series of three, five and seven steps. Among the American Indians there have been secret societies that have used symbols and rites something like our own. Once was when these fragments and hundreds more like them out of antiquity were accepted as certain proof that Freemasonry has existed from time immemorial. This cannot be disproved but a more reasonable reading of the facts suggests to us that these were merely accidental likenesses. Masonic symbols, most of them at least, as has already been said, are natural and human, and of such a character that early mankind came upon them naturally and inevitably. There was no need that a Masonic institution exist in order that men express themselves so. Such symbols grew up out of the human mind as grass springs from the sod. The causes which create secret societies in modern times created secret societies in ancient times. Ancient fraternities and teachers of symbolism prepared the way for modern Freemasonry and contributed many elements to the making of its philosophy and ritual, but it is going too far to say that our Order can trace a straight line of ancestry back to ancient Egypt, or beyond. Looking back upon early movements of this kind the Freemason of today can say, "That which our Fraternity is now trying to do those early brethren were trying to do, and what they did helped make it possible for our Fraternity to come into existence; by studying them I can the better understand Freemasonry as it now exists."

The first of these early anticipations of Freemasonry to claim our attention, is the Men's House, of which Professor Hutton Webster has given us so exhaustive an account in his "Primitive Secret Societies." According to this excellent authority the primitive tribe was in reality a secret society, at least so far as the men were concerned. At the centre of the village stood a large building; in this the unmarried men had their quarters; the chiefs and elders held their deliberations; and it was here that the boys, when they were come of age, were initiated into the secrets of the tribe. These secrets were probably the knowledge of the arts of war, of the arts of the chase, and of the revered traditions. The initiation was an arduous ordeal, barbaric in character, and sometimes so severe as to cause death. The youth who shrunk from it was sent back to live with women and children. This ancient institution is of interest to us because it exhibits in a very early form the human necessity for initiation and for secret organization.

The next manifestation of what we may call the human instinct for Freemasonry (using the word here in a broad sense) occurred in the Ancient Mysteries, of which examples were found among most of the early nations. Of these the best known are the Egyptian, built up around such myths as those of Isis and Osiris; the Greek, more especially the Eleusinian; and the cult Mithraism, which gained such a hold on the Romans, especially the soldiers, as to prove a powerful rival to Christianity. These cults, as needs not be said, differed among themselves in many important respects but some things they had in common. Meetings were held in secret; the candidate was symbolically clothed; he participated in an acted allegorical drama, the centre of which was a dying and a rising again; the new member was bound to his fellows by a solemn obligation; the rites and teachings had a religious foundation; and each member always stood ready to lend assistance to any fellow at any time. In some of the early cults of this kind the candidate was briefly taught a certain kind of knowledge; in a few cases the organization achieved fame as a centre of philosophical and scientific teaching, as those of Egypt for example, to which Plato, Pythagoras, and other great Greek thinkers went seeking light.

It does not appear that the early Hebrews had any such cults in their midst though the Levites, and in some cases, the Schools of the Prophets, approximated to the secret society in their forms of organization. The only famous Jewish cult, the Essenes, came at a later day. The first mention of the Essenes as a distinct sect was made a century and a half before Christ.

Essenism was a religious order, the members of which practised celibacy, taught a puritan morality, and lived in common, sharing all things equally. Their influence was so vital a leaven that it carried many of their teachings and much of their language into popular usage. "Much of the Sermon on the Mount," says one authority, "is expressed in the phraseology of the sect." Certain of their tenets, no doubt, passed over into that stream of tradition later inherited by Freemasonry but our Order did not originate with the Essenes, though some have argued in behalf of such a theory, the learned Dr. Krause, for example.

Other cults could be mentioned: the Druses of Mt. Lebanon, for example; the Druids, who flourished during the early Dark Ages; the Culdees, that fraternity of Ireland about which so little is known; the Pythagoreans, founded by the followers of Pythagoras, the Greek philosopher. It may be that Freemasonry owes something to some one of these, or, it may be, to all of them, but if so the indebtedness is too slender to warrant further discussion thereon.

There is another of these obscure cults, however, about which a word may be said; we refer to the Dyonysian Artificers, a fraternity which, if our very slender sources of information are to be trusted, was organized about the rites and emblems of architecture. According to Strabo, an old Greek historian, and fairly reliable, this fraternity originated in Greece but later migrated to Phoenicia, which lies just west of the country inhabited by the Hebrews. This fraternity, it appears, soon possessed such a monopoly of the building trade in that country, that when King Hiram of Tyre, a great Phoenician, undertook to build for King Solomon the latter's royal temple at Jerusalem, lodges of the Dyonoysian Artificers were sent to Jerusalem to do the work. Afterwards these Artificers migrated into Italy, whence they carried with them traditions concerning the building of Solomon's Temple, some of which, it is believed, may have been preserved until this day. Also, it is worthy of note, the Dyonysian Artificers probably had something to do with the rise of the Builders' Collegia in Rome. Of these Collegia more must be said.

A Collegium ("Collegia" is the plural) was an association of not less than three men, organized for some specific purpose under the laws of Rome. They began to be fanned during the first century of our era, and they reached their greatest development during the fourth century. Most of them were Burial Clubs, and existed in order to give the member a respectable interment; others were strictly religious in nature, as in the case of the first Christian societies, which were Collegiate in form; others still were strictly social in nature, like our Shrine; and then there were a great many of miscellaneous character about which nothing need be said. The Collegia which interest us most were those organized by men engaged in the building trades. Each branch of that trade had its Collegia, and these Collegia, aside from their purely fraternal and charitable features, no doubt preserved the secrets of architecture. Members were received by ballot; were admitted through an initiation ceremony based on religion and much like our own; there was a common treasury to which each member paid annual dues; each member was placed under oath to keep the secrets of the organization; and the ritual was usually based on a religious myth which had to do with the death and the rising again of some god. The Masonic reader, as we need not say, already sees the points of similarity with modern Freemasonry and we may agree with all our Masonic scholars in looking upon the Collegia as the Freemasonic lodges of their day and as having contributed much to that long stream of evolution which culminated in our modern Fraternity.

When the Barbarians swept down upon Rome the Collegia, like all other organizations and institutions in the Empire, suffered beyond description; most of them went out of existence entirely and others lingered on, changed beyond description. Among those that suffered most were the architectural bodies, for, according to such slender evidence as we possess, they were almost completely destroyed, so that it appeared that architecture, or Masonry as it used to be called, was a lost art. And yet, at the end of the Dark Ages there began to appear in Europe the most marvellous buildings that have ever been erected by the wit and ingenuity of man. Who preserved the builder's intricate and difficult art during that long lapse from civilization? For a long time the historians of architecture were at a loss to explain this mystery but of late there has grown up a hypothesis which more and more claims the allegiance of learned men. It is called the Comacine Theory, and thus far the ablest and most exhaustive presentation of it has been made by a woman, Leader Scott, in her volume entitled "The Cathedral Builders." According to this reading of the matter, a guild of architects fled from the Barbarians at the time of the Roman invasion and took refuge on the fortified island of Comacina in the midst of Lake Como, which lies in Lombardy, and which region was at the time the one free place in Italy. These master builders preserved the secrets of their art and passed it on to their sons, generation after generation, until such time as the new rulers of Europe were themselves sufficiently civilized to demand suitable houses and beautiful public buildings. Then it was that the Comacini began to spread their influence about. They organized schools in which youth were taught the rudiments of letters and something of building, and they superintended the erection of walled towns, of highways, palaces, and cathedrals. As the arts of peace gained on the arts of war these builders became more and more in demand until they had spread over much of Europe, and even as far as England, and perhaps as far as Ireland. "They were the link," writes Leader Scott, "between the classic Collegia and all other art and trade guilds of the Middle Ages. They were Freemasons because they were builders of a privileged class, absolved from taxes and servitude, and free to travel about in times of feudal bondage."

As time went on through the Middle Ages, other kinds of guilds were established, as in the Roman Empire, and along with these others, the various branches of the building profession gradually became organized; quarrymen, stone-cutters, wallers, plasterers, etc., each group had its own guild. But gradually it came about, owing to causes operating at the time, which causes cannot be here explained through lack of space, that the majority of these builders' guilds became purely local in nature, and therefore stationary. The builders' organization in one city was distinct and separate from the similar organization in an adjoining city; workmen were not permitted to move about at will seeking employment because the feudal system did not permit it. Among all these organizations was one guild, descending from the Comacine Masters, which stood apart from the rest; this was the Cathedral Builders. To erect a cathedral was an art in itself which required peculiar skill and special knowledge of architecture and therefore the mere local craftsmen were unequipped to work on these and similar structures; accordingly the Cathedral Builders were exempted from the municipal and feudal restrictions and were permitted to move about from place to place. Many of our scholars believe it was from these particular guilds that Freemasonry has descended and some of them, G. W. Speth for example, believe that the word "Freemason" came into use because these builders, or "masons," were "free" to move about from town to town.

Be that as it may, it is certain that Freemasonry traces back to the medieval builders' guilds that which is most characteristic of itself, its system of symbolism organized about the arts of architecture. The Masonry of these guilds was "operative," that is, it was engaged in the actual building processes, and in that regard was fundamentally different from our own symbolical variety, which is called "speculative"; but in most other regards the modern speculative lodge is strikingly similar to the associations of operatives. Like us the Each community had its own building traditions. But operative masons had lodges, and usually a well-guarded building in which to meet; they convened in secret; they were governed by masters and wardens; members were admitted by initiation, and were taught to make themselves known to each other by grips and signs; and the candidates were instructed by a system of symbols and emblems. When a youth presented himself for membership he was carefully examined, then admitted as Apprentice, or learner, and his name was entered on the books, whence our term, "Entered Apprentice." He was then placed in charge of a Master Mason, lived perhaps in that brother's home, and remained under his tutelage for a period of years, usually seven. At the expiration of this term he was examined, he had to produce a masterpiece, and, if found worthy, was initiated as a "Fellow of the Craft," or Master Mason, the two terms being interchangeable in those days. These guilds had certain traditions sometimes kept in writing, and they used "charges" to the candidates; some of these interesting old documents are still extant, and the curious reader will find a well edited collection of them in W. J. Hughan's little book, "Ancient Charges." These documents are quaint in form, uncritical in their account of the origins of Masonry, and in many other ways on a level with their age; but in respect of morality they inculcated a standard far in advance of their times. No modern Mason has any cause to feel ashamed of this ancestry.

It would be in order now to turn to the Steinmetzen, a powerful German association of builders, or to the Companionage, a French association of travelling Masons, because all our Masonic historians believe that we owe many things to these two great fraternities; but the reader must be referred to Gould's four volume "History" for a full account of these; the restrictions of space compel us to hasten on to the causes which led in the sixteenth century to a breakup of the old builders' guilds in general and the Cathedral Builders in particular. Our attention will be confined to England because that country became the home of the evolution of Freemasonry from this time on.

A long drawn out Civil War exhausted the people in spirit and finance. The monasteries, long-time patrons of architecture, were dissolved. Puritanism came on the scene with an intense hatred for architecture and its demand for plain barn-like structures. Simon Grynaeus, a contemporary of Martin Luther, rediscovered Euclid's treatise on geometry and published it to the world, thereby "giving away" many of the trade secrets of the Masons. For these, and for many other less important reasons, the Cathedral Builders rapidly declined in power and prestige and were finally driven to engage in domestic architecture in order to make a livelihood; and to maintain their dwindling lodges they gradually came to admit members who had no intention of engaging in actual Masonic work. These latter were called "accepted" Masons, and their Masonry was called "speculative."

What led these "accepted" Masons to join the Craft? Something of a mystery hangs over the matter but it is supposed that these men, most of whom were well-to-do and some of them, like Elias Ashmole, were learned, were attracted to the fraternity by its wealth of ancient lore, its marvellous system of symbolism, its fine traditions of brotherhood, its inherent democracy, its morality, and its noble spirit. At first the Speculative Masons were in a minority; but in time, at least in the neighborhood of London, they came to equal, or even outnumber the operatives; and at last they gained complete control and transformed the whole Fraternity into a speculative system.

Before going on to narrate this story it will be wise for us here to digress a moment in order to say a word about two or three other sources from which modern speculative Masonry undoubtedly derived certain elements. I refer to the occult societies which more or less flourished in the sixteenth and seventeenth centuries such as Kabalism, Hermeticism, Rosicrucianism, etc. We owe many things to these cults; some of our writers think we owe so much that they ask us to believe that Freemasonry was created in these circles. The present writer has no desire to underestimate our indebtedness in this instance but he believes that in occultism we find tributaries rather than the principal current. The operative Masons were not occultists; the occultists were not operative Masons; how then did the former come to be influenced by the latter? This is still a moot question but there are good reasons to believe that the non-operative Masons who were accepted in the seventeenth century were, many of them, more or less attached to schools of occultism, and that they brought some of it with them when they entered the Order. The reader who feels a keen interest in the matter is referred to such writers as Albert Pike and A.E. Waite and to the scholars who contributed to the Transactions of the Quatuor Coronate Lodge of Research. All these men, especially the mystical and erudite Waite, have gone into the question thoroughly and have a right to speak. A mere word about two or three of these occult groups will suffice for our present purpose.

In the first centuries of our era the Egyptian city of Alexandria was a great intellectual melting-pot. To that centre Greeks took their philosophies; Egyptians carried their mythologies; the Jews their Old Testament, along with learned interpretations thereof; members of the Mystery Cults took their religious allegories; Christians their Gospel; and the common man carried with him an unquenchable curiosity to know about things mystical, occult, magical. Men were often very learned and almost always superstitious to a degree, and miracles were expected as a matter of course. Because of this extraordinary jumbling of things not a few thinkers undertook to fashion new religions and philosophies which would include all the various cults, creeds, and theories. Out of Alexandria there came astonishing mixtures of thought; including certain occult systems, among the most prominent of which was Hermeticism.

This school traced its origin back to the so-called "Thrice Greatest Hermes," who was, it seems, in the hazy beginnings of Egyptian mythology, bookkeeper to the other deities. About this Hermes myth these occultists wove a mass of legend, theosophy and magic, all of which was set forth under a rich veil of symbolism. Just what these men were intending to say or to do by means of all this it is not possible or necessary for us to say, but it does concern us that Hermeticism lasted long in the world, that it exerted a wide influence, that much of it was inherited by later schools, and that many of its symbols, such as the square and compass, triangle, oblong square, gauge, plumb-line, circle with parallel lines, etc., have found place in the system of Masonic symbolism. It may be that a few of these came to us direst from Hermeticism through the speculative Masons who were accepted by Masonic lodges before the era of the first Grand Lodge.

Kabalism is another school of magic and theosophy to which Masonic historians have paid attention. For some time prior to Jesus many Jewish scholars were in the habit of interpreting the Old Testament allegorically and mystically. A number of Jewish rabbis who found their way to Alexandria carried these speculations with them, and later fused them with a number of pagan and possibly Christian elements wherefrom they built up the strange system called Kabalism. Needless to say many symbols were employed in the four or five books accepted as authoritative (the word "Kabala" means "accepted") and among these a Mason would be interested in the Lost Name, Solomon's Temple, the Shekinah, etc. Kabalism existed in out-of-the-way places during the Dark Ages and was brought into Europe by Arabian metaphysicians; falling upon a credulous and magic loving age it was eagerly studied, even by Christian theologians, and it is very probable that certain of its speculations and a few of its symbolisms found their way into the stream of Masonic traditions. At any rate Masonic historians so believe, and most of them number it among secondary Masonic sources.

Out of the mingled currents of Hermeticism and Kabalism was born, early in the seventeenth century, another school of occultism known as Rosicrucianism and so named, probably, because its members were called "Brethren of the Rosy Cross." What was meant by this name is now lost. The Bible of this cult was a strange German book issued in 1614 and called "Fama Fraternitas," which volume has been attributed by some scholars, Dr. Begeman for example, to a Protestant theologian, Dr. Andrea by name. The "Fama" declared that Rosicrucians were of the Protestant faith, honored king and country, sought the Philosopher's Stone, and searched for the Elixir of Life. One encounters familiar symbols in Rosicrucian pages, such as the globe, the compasses, square, triangle, level, plummet, etc. It is difficult and often impossible to follow out the traces of this esoteric cult but it appears that its waters often washed the Masonic shores; just how much we are indebted to it must be left to future scholarship to decide. As yet we know so little about the whole subject that it is wise to avoid positive statements.

One is tempted to go more thoroughly into these matters. Freemasons, for some reason or other, always have been, and even now remain, peculiarly susceptible to the appeal of the occult; we have had some experience in this country during recent years that prove this. No doubt a learned dustman can find particles of gold buried away in the debris of occultism and the true gold, even in small quantities, is not to be despised; but the dangers attendant upon trifling with the magical are a heavy price to pay for what little we can gain. Those who have, with worn fingers, untangled the snarl of occult symbolism, tell us that these secret cults have been teaching the doctrine of the one God, of the brotherhood of man, and of the future life of the soul; all this is good but one doesn't need to wade through jungles of weird speculations in order to come upon teachings that one may find in any Sunday School. It behooves the wise student to walk warily; perhaps the wisest thing is to leave occultism altogether alone. Life is too short to tramp around its endless labyrinths. Moreover, there is on the surface of Freemasonry enough truth to equip any of us for all time to come.

Thus far we have rapidly traced our evolution from the beginning, down through the Roman Collegia, through the medieval guilds, into the beginnings of Speculative Masonry; we have glanced at a few of the currents of occultism from which we have received something; it is now in order to turn to the Grand Lodge era; and we can turn to it not without a sense of relief because we can, except in matters of minute detail, walk upon the solid ground of fact.

By the opening of the eighteenth century Freemasonry had almost lapsed out of existence; it was not dead but it was exceedingly dormant, and what few lodges were scattered here and there over England, Scotland and Ireland, had little in common except the name and the tradition of a great fraternity. In Scotland it came to pass that one man could make a Mason of another merely by giving him the so-called "Mason's word"; in Ireland conditions differed radically from those that obtained in England; what condition Freemasonry was in on the continent it is hard to say.

But the time for a great awakening had come and the first gleams of a new day brightened the horizon in the year 1716 when certain members of a few lodges in or about London "thought fit to cement under a Grand Master as the centre of Union and Harmony." How many of these "Old Lodges" were concerned we do not know, but Dr. James Anderson, a Presbyterian minister, whose story of the period is "the only official account we possess of the foundations of the Grand Lodge of England, and of the first six years of its history," gives us the names of four, those that met in the following places:

1. The Goose and Gridiron Ale-House. 2. The Crown Ale-House. 3. The Apple-Tree Tavern. 4. Rummer and Grapes Tavern.

To quote Anderson, whose "The New Book of Constitutions" was issued in 1738:

"They and some other old Brothers met at the said Apple-Tree, and having put into the chair the oldest Master Mason (now the Master of a Lodge) they constituted themselves a Grand Lodge Pro Tempore in due form, and forthwith revived the Quarterly Communication of the Officers of Lodges (called the GRAND LODGE) resolv'd to hold the Annual Assembly and Feast, and then to chuse a Grand Master from among themselves, till they should have the Honor of a Noble Brother at their Head.

"Accordingly, on St. John Baptist's Day, in the 3d year of King George I, A. D. 1717, the ASSEMBLY and Feast of the Free and Accepted Masons was held at the aforesaid Goose and Gridiron Ale-Hause.

"Before Dinner, the oldest Master Mason (now the Master of a Lodge) in the chair, proposed a List of proper Candidates; and the Brethren by a Majority of Hands elected Mr. Anthony Sayer, Gentleman, Grand Master of Masons (Mr. Jacob Lamball, Carpenter, Capt. Joseph Elliott, Grand Wardens) who being forthwith invested with the badges of Office and Power by the said oldest Master, and install'd, was duly congratulated by the Assembly who paid him the Homage.

"Sayer, Grand Master, commanded the Masters and Wardens of Lodges to meet the Grand Officers every Quarter in Communication, at the Place that he should appoint in the Summons sent by the Tyler."

George Payne became Grand Master in 1718 and caused "several old copies of the Gothic (i.e. manuscripts) Constitutions" to be "produced and collated," a fact which shows that they earnestly desired to adhere to the old traditions. Rev. J.T. Desaguliers was elected Grand Master in 1719, and George Payne received a second term in 1720. During the year several manuscripts - copies of the old Constitutions, probably - were burned "by some) scrupulous Brothers, that these papers might not fail into strange Hands." In 1721 Grand Lodge elected to the Grand Mastership John, Duke of Montagu, "the first of a long and unbroken line of noble Grand Masters - and the society rose at a single bound into notice and esteem." So popular did the Order become that the learned

Dr. Stokely, writing January 6, 1721, complained that "immediately upon that it took a run and ran itself out of breath through the folly of the members."

At first the Grand Lodge, the formation of which is above described, claimed no jurisdiction except over London and its immediate environs; but it was possessed of such vitality that there was nothing to stay its growth every whither. In 1721 twelve lodges were represented at the Quarterly Communication; by 1723 the number had increased to thirty. Gradually lodges outside London came into the jurisdiction and the Grand Lodge itself chartered new organizations here and there, one of which was the lodge in Madrid in 1728, the first on foreign soil.

But the growing authority of the Grand Lodge at London was not unchallenged. In 1725 the old lodge at York began to call itself a Grand Lodge. In 1729 Irish Masons instituted a Grand Lodge of their own; and the Scotch followed in 1736. Moreover, rivals sprang up in England itself so that at one time there were no fewer than four bodies operating as Grand Lodges and claiming full sovereignty as such.

One can easily lose himself in the details of the story of all this Masonic organization and re-organization; in the present connection we can safely ignore all except the account of the famous schism of 1753. A number of Masons in London, mostly Irish, rebelled against the Grand Lodge there and finally set up a Grand Lodge of their own, averring that the older body had departed from many, ancient landmarks. Calling themselves "Ancient" Masons they dubbed the others the "Moderns" and undertook a vigorous campaign which was, engineered by an exceedingly able man, Lawrence Dermott, who served as secretary of the "Ancient" Grand Lodge for thirty years and was tireless in furthering its aims. It was he who published in 1756 its first book of laws, called "Ahiman Rezon," which title is supposed by some to mean "Worthy Brother Secretary." Dermott adopted the expedient of army lodges whereby men in service in every part of the world could be inducted into the Fraternity, and this in itself added power to the "Ancients," or Atholl Masons as they also came to be called, owing to the fact that the Duke of Atholl was made Grand Master.

For a long time there was constant strife between the two camps, but by the first decade of the nineteenth century overtures began to be made by one Grand Lodge to the other committees were appointed, and the spirit of unity began to win its way. In 1813 a great Lodge of Reconciliation was held, at which meeting there were 641 lodges of the so-called "Moderns" represented, and 359 "Ancients." From this famous assembly Masonry emerged cleansed of all its feuds, united and triumphant.

Some time during the first quarter of the eighteenth century Masonry was introduced into America; at least, the earliest known records bear such a date. With the organization of the Grand Lodge in England Masonry received a new impetus and spread rapidly over the colonies, north, south and west. Some American lodges were organized under warrant from the "Moderns," others under the "Ancients," and this fact in itself accounts for some of the variations in our rituals and customs. Washington, Lafayette, Franklin, Alexander Hamilton, Chief Justice Marshall, such were the names in early nineteenth century American Masonry; and from Revolutionary days until the present when such men as Theodore Roosevelt are proud to own their affiliation, the Craft has drawn to itself many of the noblest leaders of the nation. The Order played a secret but important part in the Revolution, made itself vitally felt in the terrible years of the Civil War, and at the present labors without fear, fatigue, or failure in behalf of such principles as form the very structure of our nation. What Masonry is to mean in the future no man knows, nor can know, but it is still filled with undying youth, and it so happens that in the very autumn in which this is being written a great Masonic Service Association has been launched by a large number of Grand Lodges through their representatives at Cedar Rapids, Iowa. Of all these things it is impossible to write; nor is it possible to say anything of the Higher Grades, or of the work of the great individuals who have played such a part in the formation of American Masonry, and through it of the nation; such names as Albert Pike, Theodore Sutton Parvin, Albert Mackey, and many others of similar repute, would shine in any roster of great men.

Freemasonry is in its very nature profoundly religious but it is not a church, for, though it is friendly to all churches that preach the Fatherhood of God, the Brotherhood of Man, and the Immortality of the Soul, it teaches no theological dogmas of its own. It is not a political organization, whatever its enemies may allege, but it is vitally interested in the public life of the land and never sleeps in its efforts to keep American governmental life as pure as possible. It preaches no program of reform but nevertheless lends itself to every effort made to lift the burdens of life from the common people, and it evermore holds before its membership the high ideals of service and of mutual helpfulness. It is a great body of picked men, in this country two million strong, who are bound together by sacred and serious obligations to assist each other, by means of fraternity, and through the teaching instrumentalities of ritual, to build in each man and in society at large a communal life which is not inadequately described as a Holy Temple of Human Souls.

Such, in brief, is the Story of Freemasonry. What a story it is! It began in a far fore-time in a few tiny rivulets of brotherly effort; these united into a current that swept with healing waters across the pagan centuries; many tributaries augmented its stream during the Middle Ages; and in modern times it has become a mighty river which sweeps on irresistibly. And now, if we may venture to change the figure, its halls are the homes of light and life; therein men may learn how good and pleasant it is for brethren to dwell together in unity. Well may one unclasp his shoes and uncover his head as he enters a Masonic lodge; a symbolism white with an unutterable age is there, and voices eloquent with an old, old music, and a wisdom drawn from the thought and travail of a thousand generations!

WOMAN AND FREEMASONRY
by Dudley Wright

Wise men tell us that there never has been a woman Freemason. Perhaps that is true. This question has been called to the attention of the able scholar and devoted Mason who contributes this series of articles. Can Freemasonry enlarge its borders to include women or must they forever remain outside the pale? If they are to be made Masons in literal truth in what way can we reorganize the ritual so as to eliminate certain features which might prove embarrassing to them? If they cannot be admitted into full membership in what way can the spirit and teachings of this ancient Fraternity be made available to them? Since Freemasonry began to be this has been a moot question; it is still. It will be for years to come. It is a theme of perennial interest. For this reason we are very glad indeed to give to our readers the reasoned and mature judgments of a scholar who has every right to speak on this interesting question.

RITUAL OF FREEMASONRY FOR LADIES

(The Ritual of Adoptive Masonry here given differs from that appearing in the August number of THE BUILDER. It was published in 1791, in the French language, from which it is now for the first time translated.)

FIRST DEGREE

PREPARATION OF THE LODGE AND OF THE CANDIDATE

THE SISTERS and brethren are convened in a spacious apartment, brilliantly lighted with wax candles, five of which are placed in the south, while five others are placed on a pedestal in the north, and arranged in such a manner as to illuminate a picture illustrating the angel expelling Adam from the Garden of Eden.

The Grand Master, wearing white gloves and apron, his breast decorated with a silver ladder pendant from a white ribbon, and holding a silver trowel in his right hand, takes his seat in the north part of the lodge. The Grand Inspectors, wearing white aprons and gloves are placed at right angles to the Grand Master. One has a silver hammer and the other a miniature silver Tower of Babel, pendant from white ribbons from their breasts.

(The northern situation of the Grand Master is in accordance with the traditional belief that this is the most appropriate situation for one whose duty it is to impart knowledge.)

The sisters and brethren wear embroidered aprons and, during the ceremony of initiation, the former sit to right and left of the Grand Master's throne, while the latter, holding white wands in their hands, arrange themselves in an oblong, from north to south, in order to receive the candidates for initiation.

The Grand Master instructs one of the sisters (who is assisted by a brother), preferably the sister who has proposed the candidate for initiation, to see that the candidate is properly prepared. This preparation consists first of depriving her of all jewelry and money, the intention being that she shall be reminded of the fact that intellectual worth only is considered of value by the members of the Order. A white veil is then thrown over her head and, blindfolded, she is conducted by the brother to the entrance of the lodge.

MANNER OF OPENING THE LODGE AND OF INITIATING A CANDIDATE

The Grand Master commands attention by clapping his hands in a peculiar manner five times, an act which is repeated by the Inspectors. Both sisters and brethren rise and the Grand Master addressing the Junior Inspector says:

"What is the duty of every Mason?"

Answer: "To hear, to obey, to work, and to be silent."

Grand Master: "Brethren and sisters, may we hear and may we obey. Let us work and let us be silent.

All the members and visitors salute the Grand Master and intimate their obedience to his commands by clapping their hands five times.

The candidate is admitted by five taps at the door and the brother who acts as her guide hands her over to the charge of an Inspector who conducts her round the lodge and leaves her standing in front of the Senior inspector, who asks the question:

"What is the cause of this intrusion?"

Answer: "A lady desires to become a Mason."

This is communicated to the Grand Master who asks the candidate:

"Has curiosity any share in your request?"

Answer: "No."

Grand Master: "Are you willing to be rid of the prejudices common to your sex? If so, we are willing to admit you to our ranks."

Answer: "I am."

Grand Master: "In order that you may be enabled to persevere in those sentiments, brethren and sisters, assist the candidate and conduct her to the entrance of the Temple of Virtue."

The veil is then removed and the candidate is welcomed by the members of the lodge who signify their willingness to admit her into their company by striking their aprons with their hands.

The brethren with their wands then form an arch under which the candidate passes and advances by slow, measured steps to the pedestal. She kneels on a cushion and with her right hand placed on a Masonic apron, repeats the following obligation, word for word, after the Grand Master:

OBLIGATION

"In the presence of the Creator of All Things, and of the members of this lodge, and by that honor, which is the distinguishing characteristic of a virtuous woman, I promise to keep strictly and truly the secrets of Masons and Masonry under the penalty of being excluded from the company of my friends here on earth and from Paradise hereafter."

The approbation of the members is intimated by the striking of their aprons with their hands. The candidate then uses and is invested by the Grand Master with an apron and a silver ladder, and he addresses her as follows:

Grand Master: "You are now, madame, an initiated Mason and as such I can entrust you with the sign, the grip, and the pass-word. Give me the pleasure to address you as a sister and as such to salute you with the kiss of peace."

INSTRUCTION IN THE FIRST DEGREE

The principal part of this catechism is undertaken generally by the Grand Master or some other brother proficient in the science, but the original intention was that every member should, in turn, take part in the answers.

Grand Master: "What is the duty of an initiated Mason?"
Answer: "To hear, to obey, to work, and to be silent."

Grand Master: "Are you an apprenticed Mason?"

Answer: "I believe so."

Grand Master: "Are you not certain?"

Answer: "It is prudent to be doubtful of everything and certain of nothing."

Grand Master: "In what manner were you admitted into the lodge?"

Answer: "I was blindfolded."

Grand Master: "For what reason?" Answer: "To intimate that my curiosity could not be gratified, and that I could only attain to the knowledge of the sublime mysteries if possessed of the fortitude to persevere."

Grand Master: "Where were you received as an apprentice?"

Answer: "Between the Ladder of Jacob and the Tower of Babel."

Grand Master: "What does that Ladder signify?"

Answer: "Its meaning is mysterious, but, so far as I can understand it, I conceive that the duty of all mankind is indicated by it."

Grand Master: "Will you explain your meaning?"

Answer: "It is emblematic of prudence and justice."

Grand Master: "Into how many parts is the figure divided?"

Answer: "Five."

Grand Master: "What are they?"

Answer: "Two external sides and three internal steps."

Grand Master: "Be more explicit and inform the lodge in what manner prudence and justice are depicted."

Answer: "Prudence is indicated by one of the external parts, which is held to illustrate the veneration and love due to our Creator. His justice is indicated by the other side, which is also held to be symbolical of the attention and love due to our neighbors."

Grand Master: "What do the steps indicate?"

Answer: "The moral virtues, the practice of which will lead us to immortality."

Grand Master: "What does the Tower of Babel represent?"

Answer: "The pride of the children of the earth. The only presevative against that destructive passion is the inner exercise of temperance."

Grand Master: "How do you arrive at this knowledge in Masonry?"

Answer: "Through the Arch."

Grand Master: "What does that Arch represent?"

Answer: "Unity and Strength."

Grand Master: "Give the sign of an initiated Mason to your sister."

(The forefinger and thumb of the right hand are applied to the left ear of the sister.)

Grand Master: "Give her the salute also."

(A salute on the left cheek.)

Grand Master: "Give me the pass-word."

Answer: "Amice."

Grand Master: "What does that word denote?"

Answer: "Benevolence."

Grand Master: "What is meant by Benevolence?"

Answer: "Masonry."

Grand Master: "What is worn by an initiated Mason?"

Answer: "The symbol of Jacob's Ladder."
Grand Master: "Whither will that ladder lead?"

Answer: "To felicity"

Grand Master: "And what is the duty of an initiated Mason?"

Answer: "To hear, to obey, to work, and to be silent."

SECOND DEGREE

PREPARATION OF THE LODGE

The brethren and sisters who have already passed the Second degree only are permitted to be present for the purpose of forming a lodge for the admission of the candidate. They assemble in a convenient room, in the center of which is placed a tree, on which is fruit.

The only light in the room is supplied by means of spirits of wine and salt, placed on a pedestal. On the east side of the lodge is a star; on the west a painting of death; on the north a representation of Adam and Eve in the Garden of Eden; while in the south is placed a buffet with wines, sweet-meats, etc.

The officers, brethren and sisters are placed in the same order as in the previous degree.

A silver chain of considerable length and a bracelet engraved with the words "Virtue and Silence," are placed on the pedestal.

PREPARATION AND INSTRUCTION OF THE CANDIDATE

The initiate is conducted by a brother or sister to an ante-room, where she is received by the Inspector, who hands to her a white ribbon, which is fastened round her right arm, by means of which she is led into the lodge. Previously to this, however, the Inspector asks her if she is willing to submit to the trial belonging to the second degree, that of Companion, and a reply in the affirmative being received, she is blindfolded and handed over to the care of the Brother Inspector, who notifies the fact to the lodge by giving five shouts.

Grand Master: "What is your request?"

Answer: "An initiated Mason is desirous of being admitted as a Companion and offers herself voluntarily for the purpose of undergoing the trials necessary to attain to the knowledge of the Second degree."

Grand Master (to Candidate): "Know that in order that you may attain to this dignity to which you aspire it is essential that you display fortitude, for if the least fear is evinced by you, it may cause you to be rejected."

(To Inspector): "Lead the candidate to the pedestal in order that she may behold the danger of her situation" (at this moment the veil is removed). (To Candidate):

"Behold the trials to which you are exposed. Travel towards the west and behold the nature of your existence and remember that the charms of beauty will not avail when your sun is set. The picture now before you is a true representation of what you must come to. May this picture never be effaced from your memory. As there is no true picture without a shadow, observe in the east a light: that is emblematical of the star of life."

The candidate is then conducted to the pedestal where she is told to kneel.

Grand Master: "Have you infringed your vow as an initiated Mason?"

Answer: "I have not."

Grand Master: "Will you persist in keeping inviolate the obligation you are about to be entrusted with, as well as the one you have taken already?"

Answer: "I hope so to do."

The Grand Master then places a silver chain around her neck, saying:

"You are not, sister, to suppose that this chain is an emblem of slavery; on the contrary, it points to the union of friendship which, as a Companion, you are to evince for all members of the Order."

OBLIGATION

"I promise by the penalty attaching to my former vow never to speak of the secrets of this degree, to be a friend to the whole of the human race, to abstain from eating the core of apples, to wear the bracelet of the Order, to sleep with it this night, and never to reveal the secret which that bracelet implies."

The candidate then rises and is divested of the chain and ribbon, and invested with the bracelet of the Order.

Grand Master: "Notwithstanding your vows, I anoint your lips with the seal of discretion, that being the only security in Masonry. Receive likewise this fruit, refresh yourself with it, but reject the core: you will then become One of Us."

The new Companion tastes the fruit, the members as a body saluting her with cries of "Eve."

The Grand Master then seats the Companion on his left and, giving the signal for silence, addresses her as follows:

"The silence of Masonry is as honorable as it is ancient; the pass-word of this degree is as ancient as the Creation, and its antiquity is proved beyond the possibility of doubt. The honor, therefore, which is attached to it, which you will hereafter experience, is beyond your comprehension at present or my power to express. You ought peculiarly to rejoice in your present situation, for many have attempted to attain to the knowledge of this degree, but have been rejected, and the disappointed candidates thus withdrawn have experienced a shame seldom known to human beings except on such humiliating occasions."

INSTRUCTION IN THE SECOND DEGREE

Grand Master: "What is the duty of a Companion Mason?"

Answer: "To obey, to work, to hear, and to be silent."

Grand Master: "Are you a Companion?"

Answer: "Give me an apple and I will prove it."

Grand Master: "How were you received as a Companion?"

Answer: "By the anointing of my lips and by tasting the fruit."

Grand Master: "With what were your lips anointed?"

Answer: "The seal of discretion."

Grand Master: "What is the meaning of this sign?"

Answer: "It is to teach Us that the lips of Masons are never to be opened to reveal our mysteries except to those who, upon examination, prove to be One of Us."

Grand Master: "What does the fruit signify?"

Answer: "It implies friendship as we all partook of the same upon our admission to this degree."

Grand Master: "As you assemble as sisters what is its further significance?"

Answer: "The essence of stability."

Grand Master: "In what way?"

Answer: "In our having virtue as the basis of our superstructure."

Grand Master: "How did you arrive to the dignity of a Companion?"

Answer: "By means of a tree."

Grand Master: "Where was the tree?"

Answer: "In a garden."

Grand Master: "What was the name given to this garden?"

Answer: "Eden, the same as that in which Adam and Eve were placed at the Creation."

Grand Master: "In what part of the garden was the tree, to which you allude, placed?"

Answer: "In the center of it."

Grand Master: "By what name was it called?"

Answer: "The tree of knowledge of good and evil."

Grand Master: "By what was the garden bounded?"

Answer: "By a river."

Grand Master: "What does this river represent?"

Answer: "The stream is indicative of the rapidity of the human passions, which are to be restrained only by Masonry."

Grand Master: "What became of Adam and Eve?"

Answer: "They were expelled from the garden."

Grand Master: "For what reason?"
Answer: "For their disobedience to the commands of their Maker they forfeited their inheritance."

Grand Master: "What lesson is inculcated by their conduct?"

Answer: "It teaches us that should any one of us violate the vows we have taken as Companions the consequence will be that we shall be refused admission to the Order."

Grand Master: "Why is a Companion forbidden to eat the cores of apples?"

Answer: "Because the core is supposed to be the seed of the forbidden fruit."

Grand Master: "I present you with this apple and desire that you will prove to this lodge that you are a Companion Mason."

The Companion takes the apple, from which she abstracts the core, which she places on the pedestal.

Grand Master: "Why was the serpent introduced into the garden?"

Answer: "The serpent is an emblem of eternity as well as the symbol of the origin of evil."

Grand Master: "Why is this emblem placed in so conspicuous a part of the lodge?"

Answer: "As we are at present only in a state of probation it is a monitor to us to be diligent in our vocation so that we may merit by our conduct here a greater degree of happiness beyond."

Grand Master: "Why should you be reminded of the origin of evil?"

Answer: "In order that we may recognize the necessity of seeking for happiness."

Grand Master: "Where is happiness to be found?"

Answer: "In Masonry."

Grand Master: "What is the principal aim of Masons?"

Answer: "To make each other happy."
Grand Master: "What is the duty of a Companion Mason?"

Answer: "To obey, to work, to hear, and to be silent."

At the conclusion of the meeting a supper is provided and when the Companions are seated the Grand Master calls upon the newly-admitted Companion to rise, when he addresses her as follows:

"Before you partake of the refreshment provided in honor of your reception, it is necessary that the mysteries of the degree to which you have been admitted should be explained to you. The representation of death is that of the state of man after his fall, owing to the lack of discretion in the female who was created to be his companion in Paradise. As the oracles of truth have declared the seed of the woman shall bruise the serpent's head, but as the day of wrath is also declared to be accompanied by a day of mercy, I therefore now cordially welcome you into this second degree, that of felicity, in the hope that the present company will be to you as a second Paradise. From this day we admit you to our table and request your participation in our refreshments, which are emblematical of the tree of life and of the essence of Masonry."

THIRD DEGREE

The Third degree in Masonry being regarded as of the highest importance, it is very rarely granted and the ceremony is worked only on particular and special occasions. It is regarded as the highest indiscretion to entrust any but the most worthy with secrets and favors which are the property only of the worthiest of the sex.

The Companion who aspires to the Third degree must be proposed at the last but one of the two lodges preceding that when she desires to be admitted. This condition is obligatory and can on no account be dispensed with. The object of the proposition being considered at two meetings of the lodge is to give ample opportunity for any objection against the candidate being brought forward, void that every member of the lodge may be made acquainted with the proposition, notice of the proposal is sent to every member of the lodge.

At the second meeting a ballot is taken for the candidate, and if in her favor the Grand Master requests the member who proposed the Companion to desire her attendance at the next meeting. If the ballot is not in her favor the proposal cannot be made again.

OPENING OF THE LODGE

The temple in which this degree is conferred is generally reserved for this special purpose. The tapestry and decorations, however, are of so costly a character that many lodges have to resort to the expedient of having them represented on canvas.

The temple is brilliantly illuminated. At the north end of the room is depicted a rainbow, which extends from the eastern to the western extremities, and in the center is a representation of the sun, encompassed by the moon and stars. On the west side of the temple Europe is represented by a lady in a very rich habit of several colors, seated between two crossed cornucopias, the one filled with all kinds of grain and the other filled with black and white grapes. She holds a miniature temple in her right hand and, with the forefinger of the left hand, she points to representations of scepters and crowns, a horse amid trophies of arms, and a book with an owl seated above it. Several musical instruments are placed close to the picture, as well as a pallet and pencils. Adjacent is a representation of Noah's Ark, resting on a mount, with the dove entering it with an olive branch in its mouth. Jacob's Ladder, reaching from earth to heaven, with angels ascending and descending upon it, is also depicted.

Africa is represented by a blackamoor woman, almost naked, with an elephant's head for a crest, a necklace of corals and coral earrings, and a scorpion by the side of her ear. She holds in her right hand a cornucopia, while ears of corn are in her left hand. A fierce lion stands by her on one side, while a viper and a serpent are on the other.

In the east Asia is represented by a female clad in a rich embroidered vestment and wearing a garland of various flowers and fruits. She holds in her right hand branches with sprigs of cassia, pepper, and cloves, and in her left hand a smoking censer, while by her side is a kneeling camel. Near by is a model or picture of the Tower of Babel and an angel with a trowel in his hand preventing the sons of Nimrod from proceeding with that structure. There is also represented the town of Gomorrah in flames with Lot's wife transformed into a pillar of salt.

America is represented by a naked woman of tawny aspect, having a loose veil on her shoulders and wearing round her body an ornament of feathers of divers colors. She holds in one hand a bow; on her left is a human head pierced with an arrow, a lizard lying on the ground by her feet.

A pedestal covered with an embroidered cloth is placed in the center of the temple. The subjects of the embroidered work are representations of the sacrifice of Isaac by Abraham, which is on the surface of the pedestal, while on the part which hangs in front of the pedestal is a picture of the pit into which Joseph was cast by his brethren. A gold salvar is placed on the pedestal, which holds a silver box which encloses the form of a human heart with tools wherewith to shape it. A red velvet cushion with gold tassels is placed on the carpet near to the center of the saloon.

The officers of this degree consist only of the Grand Master and his Deputy, the latter holding a naked sword in his right hand during the ceremony. The jewel of the Third degree is a sword.

Every member on initiation is presented with a silver trowel which is worn afterwards on the left breast, and admission into the lodge is refused unless the member displays this jewel.

The Grand Master is placed in the north part of the lodge, the Deputy near to the pedestal, while the rest of the assembly are placed in a oblong running from north to south.

The candidate is received in an ante room by the sister who proposed her, by whom she is blindfolded and conducted to the door of the temple.

MODE OF RECEPTION

The candidate being placed comfortably and every preparation for the ceremony of reception being made, the Deputy Grand Master commands attention and order by presenting the sword, the emblem of his office, to the Grand Master, who draws his trowel across the point.

The Deputy Grand Master then perambulates the lodge exacting the same compliment from every one present. After this is done he takes his accustomed seat, and when his sword has been placed in an erect position, the Grand Master declares that the lodge is formed and that the candidate may enter. The candidate is conducted to the left of the Grand Master's chair, when she is informed that the dignity of this degree is so great that she will not be blindfolded during any part of the proceedings in order that she may be fully cognizant of its solemnity. The silver ladder which is worn by the Grand Master is then taken from his breast and placed on the carpet in front of him.

Grand Master: "Sister Companion, ascend the Ladder of Jacob."

(This is done in the usual manner.)

Grand Master: "What is the position of a sister?"

Answer: "At the summit of felicity."

Grand Master: "Take off the candidate's shoes and let her kneel at the altar of Isaac."

Then, addressing the candidate, he says:

"It is in consideration of your merit that you are placed in this position, for you are about to receive the highest honor it is in our power to confer. You have become One of Us; now place your hand on this salver and be made perfect by repeating the promise to continue in your perseverance."

The sword is now taken from its position and held by the Deputy Grand Master over the candidate's head, while she repeats the following obligation:

"I promise in the presence of the Masons now assembled, and by the sword now held over my head, that I will not divulge the secrets of Masonry, neither what I now know nor what shall be communicated to me, in consequence of this present undertaking, except to those who have already taken this obligation. "I promise also to protect and succor every one now present on all, and every occasion, according to the ability granted to me by Providence.

"I promise these things upon my word and honor. If I fail, may shame and infamy be my portion and may I be pointed at as unworthy of the respect and esteem inseparably attendant upon worthy Masons."

The point of the sword is then presented to the candidate and is kissed by her, when she is commanded to rise.

Grand Master: "It is required of every sister on admission to this degree that a present be made by her to the lodge in return for the favor conferred. You will be assisted in your choice by the Deputy Grand Master, but your own industry will, no doubt, produce the proof of your ingenuity which will be worthy of our acceptance."

The Deputy Grand Master then hands to her a box of tools and superintends the work which has been previously decided upon.

At this point refreshments are frequently introduced, after which the candidate produces the model of a heart which is formally examined by all the members of the lodge.

Grand Master: "A heart has been produced. Sister, you have consummated the great mystery of Masons. The heart is the great secret of Masonry. Our science has no other object save to regulate the passions. In a state of nature the heart is cruel and ungovernable. Our art, as Masons, effects the change, and we become the reverse of that inhospitable condition. We are as you have experienced kind and cheerful, meek and humane. Advance and receive the reward due to your work and skill. You are invested with this trowel as the key to the Third degree. This will admit you to our assemblies and now, at this particular moment, demands from us our secrets. The sign of this degree is given by drawing the trowel across the point of the sword, and then kissing the point of the sword, as at your reception. The pass-word of this degree is Esther.

The Grand Master then delivers the following address to the candidate:

"Sister: Your admission into this degree having made you on an equality with us all, it only now remains for me to describe and explain to you the symbols on the tapestry, which will conclude the ceremony of reception into this degree. Every blessing that we enjoy is derived from the Providence of our Creator, and this Providence is fittingly depicted by the sun, moon and stars. The rainbow which encompasses these luminaries is to remind us that vice once caused the world to be deluged and that our conduct as members of this Society is to be such as not to incur the repetition of the divine vengeance.

"The Ark of Noah is introduced for the express purpose of proving that the faithful Mason will always be provided for, let the winds, the waves, and the storms of the world rage ever so high. A place of refuge will never be wanting for the wife, the virtuous and the good. The Tower of Babel is emblematic of the false strength of those who are deficient in the science of Masonry, and the messenger with the trowel indicates that one moment of divine direction can put to nought and confusion the works of men. The sacrifice of Abraham is a proof that no temporal enjoyment should supersede the supreme dictates and that when our duty requires us to act we should acquiesce willingly in the divine will. The sleep of Jacob is a similitude of our condition after death and his after conduct of the respect due to the Creator from the sons and daughters of mortality. The city of Gomorrah in flames is presented to our view and shows the inevitable destruction of the vicious and the transformation of Lot's wife is at once applicable to what your position would have been had your inclinations prevented you from aspiring to this dignity. The pit into which Joseph was cast by his brethren would also have been applicable to your condition, had not your merits prevented your refusal at the ballot, for, in that case, your situation would have been like to that of Joseph, as not only would you be absent from your friends at this gathering, but you would have the mortifying reflection of knowing that you had been rejected.

"In order to demonstrate the universality of our science, representations of the four quarters of the globe are introduced. Europe is depicted as a lady in a very rich habit, and the various ornaments that surround her are emblematic of her arts and arms generally and show that she is first in point of consequence and the principal part of the world. Asia is depicted by a heroine wearing a garland of flowers and fruits, thus intimating that this quarter of the globe produces delightful things necessary for human life, as shown by the garment in which she is decked, particularly the profuseness of the rich materials in which it abounds; the bundle of spices in her right hand and the distribution of them to other parts of the world; the censer holds some of the pleasant- smelling gum which continent produces; while the camel is an animal peculiar to this region. Africa is represented by an almost naked woman, thus showing that the continent does not abound in materials for clothing; while the elephant's head, the lion, the viper, and the serpent are characteristic of the animals having their habitation there. America is depicted also by a naked woman, as showing the condition of the earliest inhabitants. The bow and quiver denote that the natives live by hunting; the human head pierced by an arrow indicates that many are cannibals; while the lizard on the ground is an animal inimical to the human race.

"In this manner we communicate the knowledge derived from the mode of reception of candidates to this degree, and thus, you will, in turn, communicate it to others.

CATECHISM OF THE THIRD DEGREE

Grand Master: "What is the duty of a Mason?"

Answer: "To work, to hear, to obey, and to be silent."

Grand Master: "How long is it since you reached this degree?"

Answer: "Seven months and more."

Grand Master: "Who assisted you in your benevolent undertaking?"

Answer: "One who was well conversant with the degree."

Grand Master: "By what name do you distinguish him?"

Answer: "The Deputy Grand Master."

Grand Master: "Who presided in the lodge on that occasion?"

Answer: "The Grand Master."

Grand Master: "Give further proof of your attainment."

Answer: "I know how to ascend the Ladder of Jacob." (Reference is here made to the plant bearing that name which will be known to students of Botany.)

Grand Master: "Probably the Iadder to which you refer is the ladder of the novitiate."

Answer: "The construction is materially different."

Grand Master: "Describe the ladder which you have ascended."

Answer: "The foundation is on the earth and it ascends to felicity. The rungs are at equal distance so as to form regular steps to the summit."

Grand Master: "What are the materials of which this ladder is composed?"

Answer: "Such as have existed from time immemorial and such as will exist to the end of time."

Grand Master: "What name is given to the base?"

Answer: "The footstool of the Almighty."

Grand Master: "How many steps are there?"

Answer: "They are innumerable."

Grand Master: "How were you enabled to take the first step?"

Answer: "By the exercise of sensibility." Grand Master: "What is this exercise of sensibility?"

Answer: "The union of souls truly noble."

Grand Master: "What principle does it teach?"

Answer: "That as I had fought and obtained happiness, so it is my duty to communicate it to others."

Grand Master: "What enabled you to ascend the second step?"

Answer: "A conscious dignity of spirit."

Grand Master: "What name does the world generally give to this principle?"

Answer: "Honor."

Grand Master: "What is its Masonic description?"

Answer: "It enjoins Masons to be strictly just where no public law can compel, to fulfil our engagements in an equitable manner, and to hold as sacred the trust reposed in us."

Grand Master: "What enabled you to ascend the third step?"

Answer: "The practice of sincerity."

Grand Master: "In what does that consist?"

Answer: "Not in deceit and guile, but in social well-being, the outcome of a generous mind."

Grand Master: "What exchange do those of a contrary principle experience?"

Answer: "They barter kindness for a shadow of joy and are deceived more than they are able to deceive."

Grand Master: "What enabled you to ascend the fourth step?"

Answer: "Experience."

Grand Master: "Its utility?"

Answer: "The control of the passions, preventing us front judging wrongfully."

Grand Master: "What are the effects of experience?"

Answer: "A conduct void of reproach and such as to merit esteem here and initiation beyond."

Grand Master: "What enabled you to ascend the fifth step?" Answer: "The knowledge I had obtained through the medium of Masonry."

Grand Master: "In what manner?"

Answer: "By the cardinal virtues which were allegorically represented in the first degree which, when united, signify wisdom."

Grand Master: "Explain this union."

Answer: "It is impossible to exercise the practice of temperance without having a due preparation of fortitude or to be in the possession of prudence without that of justice."

Grand Master: "Having ascended the step of wisdom is it necessary to delineate the remainder individually?"
Answer: "It is not, for so soon as mortals arrive at that step, the difficulties of the ascent are dissolved and the path to felicity made clear."

Grand Master: "What is the signification of Noah's Ark in the Deluge?"

Answer: "It refers to the heart of man in an uncultivated state."

Grand Master: "Why did Noah build it?"

Answer: "As a refuge for himself and family."

Grand Master: "How came he to obtain the knowledge of the approaching Deluge?"

Answer: "By attendance at the Grand Lodge of Masons over which the Creator presided."

Grand Master: "When did he enter the Ark?"

Answer: "So soon as he perceived the waters overflow the usual boundaries."

Grand Master: "What moral does this convey to us?"

Answer: "That it is our duty to frequent lodges in order that the precepts inculcated there may teach us to avoid vice, which will, when true Masonry is neglected, occasion the destruction of the world a second time."

Grand Master: "Of what material was the Ark?"

Answer: "An incorruptible wood called cedar."

Grand Master: "What lesson does the employment of this wood inculcate?"

Answer: "That the secrets of Masonry cannot be penetrated by envy and that the malice of its enemies recoils on to the breast of its propagators."

Grand Master: "What was the form of the boards of the Ark?"

Answer: "Every one was placed on a true level."

Grand Master: "The intent of this form?"

Answer: "To prove the quality of Masons and that their unity is the mainspring of their happiness."

Grand Master: "Why is the Tower of Babel introduced into the lodge?"

Answer: "As a warning against pride, which is totally at variance with the genuine dictates of the science."

Grand Master: "To whom did it owe its origin?"

Answer: "The rebellious Nimrod."

Grand Master: "What was his object in erecting so high a structure?"

Answer: "To create for himself a name among men and to make himself equal to God."

Grand Master: "How long was the building carried on?"

Answer: "Until it pleased the Creator to frustrate his design by the introduction of foreign languages the use of which threw the workmen out, in consequence of which they separated, left their work and travelled and finally settled in various parts of the world."

Grand Master: "What became of the edifice?"

Answer: "Being deserted by the human race, in process of time it became the habitation of wild beasts."

Grand Master: "What lesson is to be derived from this incident?"

Answer: "To give respect to the promises of God, to place our whole confidence in Him alone, to divest ourselves of false pride, and to work, having truth for our foundation and wisdom for our superstructure."

Grand Master: "Is there not a further lesson to be derived?"

Answer: "It is that a lodge is badly formed whenever concord and obedience are absent, and that when such conditions prevail it will inevitably fall into confusion."

Grand Master: "What lesson is inculcated by the rainbow?"

Answer: "That harmony prevails in a well-conducted lodge."

Grand Master: "What does the town in flames represent?"

Answer: "The horror which every good Mason feels at the recollection of the abominable crime that brought the fire from heaven."

Grand Master: "What does the sleep of Jacob represent?"

Answer: "The peace and tranquility in the breast of every worthy Mason."

Grand Master: "Why is an initiate deprived of light at her reception?"

Answer: "To convey to her the darkness of the uninitiated in respect to Masonry."

Grand Master: "Why do we assemble in lodges?"

Answer: "Because as often as we meet we renew our friendship."

Grand Master: "Is there any other inducement?"

Answer: "That we may communicate to each other our secrets."

Grand Master: "What is the duty of a Mason outside the lodge?"

Answer: "To work to hear, to obey, and to be silent."

The answers to the first and last questions in the catechisms of the three degrees should receive particular attention. They are as follows:

First: Hear. Obey. Work. Silent. Second: Obey. Work. Hear. Silent. Third: Work. Hear. Obey. Silent.

Hence, the primary duty of an initiate is to hear; that of a Companion, to obey; and that of a fully-admitted Mason, to work; but of members of all degrees, to be silent.

In concluding the catechism the Grand Master demands the compliment to the sword as at the reception, and the members are dismissed with the words:

"The lodge is perfect and may it ever so remain. As we met so let us part, with goodwill to all. We congratulate one another. Let us reverence the jewel of the Order and depart in peace."

IN THE INTERESTS OF THE BRETHREN
by Rudyard Kipling

I was buying a canary in a bird shop when he first spoke to me and suggested that I should take a less highly colored bird. "Color's all in the feeding," said he. "Unless you know how to feed 'em, it goes. You'll excuse me, but canaries are one of my hobbies."

He passed out before I could thank him. He was a middle-aged man with gray hair and a short dark beard, rather like a Sealyham terrier in silver spectacles. For some reason his face and his voice stayed in my mind so distinctly that, months later, when I jostled against him on a platform crowded with an Angling Club going to the Thames, I recognized, turned and nodded.

"I took your advice about the canary," I said.

"Did you? Good!" he replied heartily over the rod-case on his shoulder, and was parted from me by the crowd.

A YEAR ago I turned into a tobacconist's to have a badly stopped pipe cleaned out.

"Well! Well! And how did the canary do?" said the man behind the counter. We shook hands, and "What's your name?" we both asked together.

His name was Lewis Holroyd Burges, of "Burges and Son," as I might have seen above the door - but Son had been killed in Egypt. His beard was blacker and his hair whiter than it had been, and the eyes were sunk a little.

"Well! Well! To think," said he, "of one man in all these millions turning up in this curious way, when there's so many who don't turn up at all-eh?" (It was then he told me of Son Lewis's death and why the boy had been christened Lewis.) "There's not much left for middle-aged people just at present. Even one's hobbies-" he broke off for a breath. "We used to fish together. And the same with canaries! We used to breed 'em for color-deep orange was our specialty. That's why I spoke to you, if you remember, but I've sold all my birds. Well! Well! And now we must locate your trouble."

He bent over my erring pipe and dealt with it skilfully as a surgeon. A soldier came in, said something in an undertone, received a reply, and went out. "Many of my clients are soldiers nowadays, and a number of 'em belong to the Craft," said Mr. Burges. "It breaks my heart to give them the tobaccos they ask for. On the other hand, not one man in five thousand has a tobacco palate. Preference, yes. Palate, no. Here's your pipe. It deserves better treatment than it's had. There's a procedure, a ritual, in all things.

Any time you're passing by again, I assure you, you will be most welcome. I've one or two odds and ends that may interest you."

I left the shop with me rarest of all feelings on me - that sensation which is only youth's right - that I had made a friend. A little distance from the door I was accosted by a wounded man who asked for "Burgess." The place seemed to be known in the neighborhood.

I found my way to it again, and often after that, but it was not till my third visit that I discovered Mr. Burges held a half interest in Ackman and Permit's, the great cigar importers, which had come to him through an uncle whose children now lived almost in the Cromwell Road, and said that uncle had been on the Stock Exchange.

"I'm a shopkeeper by instinct," said Mr. Burges. "I like the ritual of handling things. The shop has always done us well. I like to do well by the shop."

It had been established by his grandfather in 1827, but the fittings and appointments were at least half a century older. The brown and red tobacco and snuff jars, with Crowns, Garters, and names of forgotten mixtures in gold leaf, the polished "Oronoque" tobacco barrels on which favored customers sat, the cherry-black mahogany counter, the delicately moulded shelves, the reeded cigar-cabinets, the German-silver mounted scales, and the Dutch brass roll and cake-cutter were things to covet.

"They aren't so bad," he admitted. "That large Bristol jar hasn't any duplicate to my knowledge. Those eight snuff-jars on the third shelf - they're Dollin's ware; he used to work for Wimble in Seventeen-Forty - they're absolutely unique. Is there any one in the trade now could tell you what Romano's Hollande' was? Or 'Scholten's,' or 'John's Lane'? Here's a snuff-mull of George the First's time; and here's a Louis Quinze - what am I talking of? Treize, Treize, of course - grater for making bran-snuff. They were regular tools of the shop in my grandfather's day. And who on earth to leave 'em to outside the British Museum now, I can't think!"

His pipes - I wish this were a tale for virtuosi - his amazing pipes were kept in the parlor, and this gave me the privilege of making his wife's acquaintance. One morning, as I was looking covetously at a jaracanda-wood "cigarro" - not cigar - cabinet with silver lock-plates and drawer-knobs of Spanish work, a wounded Canadian came into the shop and disturbed our happy little committee.

"Say," he began loudly, "are you the right place?"

"Who sent you?" Mr. Burges demanded.

"A man from Messines. But that ain't the point! I've got no certificates, nor papers-nothin', you understand. I left Lodge owin' 'em seventeen dollars back dues. But this man at Messities told me it wouldn't make any odds here."

"It doesn't," said Mr. Burges. "We meet tonight at 7 p.m."

The man's face fell a yard. "Hell!" said he. "But I'm in hospital - I can't get leave."

"And Tuesdays and Fridays at 3 p.m.," Mr. Burges added promptly. "You'll have to be proved, of course."

"Guess I can get by that, all right," was the cheery reply. "Toosday, then."

He limped off, beaming.

"Who might that be?" I asked.

"I don't know any more than you do - except he must be a Brother. London's full of Masons now. Well! Well! We must all do what we can these days. If you come to tea this evening, I'll take you on to Lodge afterward. It's a Lodge of Instruction."

"Delighted. Which is your Lodge?" I said, for up till then he had not given me its name.

"'Faith and Works 5837' - the third Saturday of every month. Our Lodge of Instruction meets nominally every Thursday, but we sit oftener than that now because there are so many Visiting Brethren in town." Here another customer entered, and I went away much interested in the range of Brother Burgess hobbies.

At tea-time he was dressed as for Church, and with gold pince-nez in lieu of the silver spectacles. I blessed my stars that I had thought to change into decent clothes.

"Yes, we owe that much to the Craft," he assented. "All Ritual is fortifying. Ritual's a natural necessity for mankind. The more things are upset, the more they fly to it. I abhor slovenly Ritual anywhere. By the way, would you mind assisting at the examinations, if there are many Visiting Brothers tonight? You'll find some of 'em very rusty but - it's the Spirit, not the Letter, that giveth life. The question of Visiting Brethren is an important one. There are so many of them in London now, you see; and so few places where they can meet."

"You dear thing!" said Mrs. Burges, and handed him his locket and initialed apron-case.

"Our Lodge is only just round the corner," he went on. "You mustn't be too critical of our appurtenances. The place was a garage once."

As far as I could make out in the humiliating darkness, we wandered up a mews and into a courtyard. Mr. Burges piloted me, murmuring apologies for everything in advance.

"You mustn't expect-" he was still saying when we stumbled up a porch and entered a carefully decorated anteroom hung round with masonic prints. I noticed Peter Gilkes and Barton Wilson, fathers of "Emulation" working, in the place of honor; Kneller's Christopher Wren; Dunkerley, with his own Fitz-George book-plate below and the bend sinister on the Royal Arms;

Hogarth's caricature of Wilkes, also his disreputable "Night," and a beautifully framed set of Grand Masters, from Anthony Sayer down.

"Are these another of your hobbies?" I asked.

"Not this time," Mr. Burges smiled. "We have to thank Brother Lemming for them." He introduced me to the senior partner of Lemming and Orton, whose dirty little shop is hard to find, but whose words and checks in the matter of prints are widely circulated.

"The frames are the best part of said Brother Lemming after my compliments. "There are some more in the Lodge Room. Come and look. We've got the big Desaguliers there that neatly went to Iowa."

I had never seen a Lodge Room better fitted. From mosaicked floor to appropriate ceiling, from curtain to pillar, implements to seats, seats to lights, and little carved music-loft at one end, every detail was perfect in particular kind and general design. I said what I thought many times over.

"I told you I was a Ritualist," said Mr. Burges. "Look at those carved corn-sheaves and grapes on the back of these Warden's chairs. That's the old tradition-before Masonic furnishers spoiled it. I picked up that pair in Stepney ten years ago-the same time I got the gavel." It was of old, yellowed ivory, cut all in one piece out of some tremendous tusk. "That came from the Cold Coast," he said. "It belonged to a Military Lodge there in 1794. You can see the inscription."

"If it's a fair question-" I began, how much-"

"It stood us," said Brother Lemming, his thumbs in his waistcoat pockets, "an appreciable sum of money when we built it in 1906, even with what Brother Anstruther-he was our contractor - cheated himself out of. By the way, that block there is pure Carrara, he tells me. I don't understand marbles myself. Since the war I expect we've put in - oh, quite another little sum. Now we'll go to the examination-room and take on the Brethren."

He led me back, not to the anteroom, but a convenient chamber flanked with what looked like confessional-boxes (I found out later that was what they had been when first picked up for a song near Oswestry). A few men in uniform were waiting at the far end. "That's only the head of the procession. The rest are in the anteroom," said an officer of the Lodge.

Brother Burges assigned me my discreet box, saying: "Don't be surprised. They come all shapes."

"Shaped' was not a bad description, for my first penitent was all head-bandages-escaped from an Officers' Hospital, Pentonville way. He asked me in profane Scots how I expected a man with only six teeth and half a lower lip to speak to any purpose, and we compromised on signs. The next - a New Zealander from Taranaki - reversed the process, for he was one-armed, and that in a sling. I mistrusted an enormous Sergeant-Major of Heavy Artillery, who struck me as much too glib, so I sent him on to Brother Lemming in the next box, who discovered he was a Past District Grand Officer. My last man nearly broke me down altogether. Everything seemed to have gone from him.

"I don't blame yer," he gulped at last. "I wouldn't pass my own self on my answers, but I give yer my word that so far as I've had any religion, it's been all the religion I've had. For God's sake, let me sit in Lodge again, Brother."

When the examinations were ended, a Lodge Officer came round with our aprons - no tinsel or silver-gilt confections, but heavily-corded silk with tassels and - where a man could prove he was entitled to them - levels, of decent plate. Some one in front of me tightened the belt on a stiffly silent person in civil clothes with discharge badge.

"'Strewth! This is comfort again," I heard him say. The companion nodded. The man went on suddenly: "Here! What're you doing? Leave off! You promised not to! Chuck it!" and dabbed at his companion's streaming eyes.

"Let him leak," said an Australian signaler. "Can't you see how happy the beggar is?"

It appeared that the silent Brother was a "shell-shocker" whom Brother Lemming had passed, on the guarantee of his friend and - what moved Lemming more - the threat that, were he refused, he would have fits from pure disappointment. So the "shocker" wept happily and silently among Brethren evidently accustomed to these displays.

We fell in, two by two, according to tradition, fifty of us at least, and we played into Lodge by the harmonium, which I discovered was in reality an organ of repute. It took time to settle us down, for ten or twelve were cripples and had to be helped into long and easy-chairs. I sat between a one-footed R.A.M.C. Corporal and a Captain of Territorials, who, he told me, had "had a brawl" with a bomb, which had bent him in two directions.

"But that's first-class Bach the organist is giving us now," he said delightedly. "I'd like to know him. I used to be a piano-thumper of sorts."

"I'll introduce you after Lodge," said one of the regular Brethren behind us - a fat, torpedo-bearded man, who turned out to be the local Doctor. "After all, there's nobody to touch Bach, is there?" Those two plunged at once into musical talk, which to outsiders is as fascinating as trigonometry.

"Now a Lodge of Instruction is mainly a parade-ground for Ritual. It cannot initiate or confer degrees, but is limited to rehearsals and lectures. Worshipful Brother Burges, resplendent in Solomon's Chair (I found out later where that, too, had been picked up), briefly told the Visiting Brethren how welcome they were and always would be, and asked them to vote what ceremony should be rendered for their instruction.

When the decision was announced he wanted to know whether any Visiting Brothers would take the duties of any Lodge Officers. They protested bashfully that they were too rusty. "The very reason why," said Brother

Burges, while the organ Bached softly. My musical Captain sighed and wriggled in his chair.

"One moment, Worshipful Sir." The fat Doctor rose. "We have here a musician for whom place and opportunity are needed. Only," he went on colloquially, "those organ-loft steps are a bit steep."

"How much," said Brother Burges, with the solemnity of an initiation, "does our Brother weigh?"

"Very little over eight stone," said the Brother. "'Weighed this mornin', sir."

The Past District Grand Officer, who was also Battery Sergeant-Major, waddled across, lifted the slight weight in his arms and bore it to the loft, where, the regular organist pumping, it played joyouly as a soul caught up to Heaven by surprise.

When the visitors had been coaxed to supply the necessary officers, a ceremony was rehearsed. Brother Burges forbade the regular members to prompt. The visitors had to work entirely by themselves, but, on the Battery Sergeant-Major taking a hand, he was ruled out as of too exalted rank. They floundered badly after that support was withdrawn.

The one-footed R.A.M.C. on my right chuckled.

"D'you like it?" said the Doctor to him.

"Do I? It's Heaven to me, sittin' in Lodge again. It's all comin' back now, watching their mistakes. I haven't much religion, but all I had I learned in Lodge." Recognizing me, he flushied a little as one does when one says a thing twice over in another's hearing. "Yes, 'veiled in all'gory and illustrated by symbols' - the Fatherhood of God, an' the Brotherhood of Man, an' what more in Hell do you want? ... Look at 'em!" He broke off, giggling. "See! See! They've tied the whole thing into knots. I could ha' done better myself - my one foot in France. Yes, I should think they ought to do it over again!"

The new organist covered the little confusion that had arisen with what sounded like the wings of angels.

WHEN the amateurs, rather red and hot, had finished, they demanded an exhibition-working of their bungled ceremony by Regular Brethren of the Lodge. Then I realized for the first time what word-and-gesture-perfect Ritual can be brought to mean. We all applauded, the one-footed Corporal most of all. It was a revelation.

"We are rather proud of our working, and this is an audience worth playing up to," the Doctor said.

Next the Master delivered a little lecture on the meanings of some pictured symbols and diagrams. His theme was a well-worn one, but his deep holding voice made it fresh.

"Marvellous how these old copybook headings persist," the Doctor said.

"That's all right!" the one-footed man spoke cautiously out of the side of his mouth like a boy in form. "But they're the kind of copybook headin's we shall find burnin' round our bunk in Hell. Believe me-ee! I've broke enough of 'em to know Now, h'sh!" He leaned forward, drinking it all in.

Presently Brother Burges touched on a point which had given rise to some diversity of Ritual. He asked for information. "Well, in Jamaica, Worshipful Sir," a Visiting Brother began, and explained how they worked that detail in his parts. Another and another joined in from different quarters of the Lodge (and the world), and when they were warmed the Doctor sidled softly round the walls and, over our shoulders, passed us cigarettes.

"A shocking innovation," he said as he returned to the captain-musician's vacant seat on my left. "But men can't really talk without tobacco, and we're only a Lodge of Instruction."

"An' I've learned more in one evenin' here than ten years.' The one-footed man turned round for an instant from a dark sour-looking Yeoman in spurs who was laying down the law on Dutch Ritual. The blue haze and the talk increased, while the organ from the loft blessed us all.

"But this is delightful," said I to the Doctor. "How did it all happen?"

"Brother Burges started it. He used to talk to the men who dropped into his shop when the war began. He told us sleepy old chaps in Lodge that what men wanted more than anything else was Lodges where they could sit-just sit and be happy like we are now. He was right, too. He generally is. We're learning things in the War. A man's lodge means move to him than people imagine. As our friend on your right said just now, very often Masonry's the only practical creed we've ever listened to since we were children. Platitudes or no platitudes, it squares with what everybody knows ought to be done." He sighed. "And if this war hasn't brought home the Brotherhood of Man to us all, I'm a-a Hun!"

"How did you get your visitors?" I went on.

"Oh I told a few fellows in hospital near here, at Burges's suggestion, that we had a Lodge of Instruction and they'd be welcome. And they came, And they told their friends. And they came! That was two years ago - and now we've Lodge of Instruction two nights a week, and a matinee nearly every Tuesday and Friday for the men who can't get evening-leave. Yes, it's all very curious. I'd no notion what the Craft meant - and means - till this war."

"Nor I till this evening," I replied.

"Yet it's quite natural if you think. Here's London - all England - packed with the Craft from all over the world, and nowhere for them to go. Why, our weekly visiting attendance for the last four months averaged just under a hundred and forty. Divide by four - call it thirty-five Visiting Brethren a time. Our record's seventy-one, but we have packed in as many as eighty-four at banquets. You can see for yourself what a potty little hole we are!"

"Banquets, too!" I cried. "It must cost like all sin. May the Visiting Brethren-"

The Doctor laughed. "No, a Visiting Brother may not."

"But when a man has had an evening like this he wants to-"

"That's what they all say. That makes our difficulty. They do exactly what you were going to suggest, and they're offended if we don't take it."

"Don't you?" I asked.

"My dear man - what does it come to? They can't all stay to banquet. Say one hundred suppers a week - fifteen quid - sixty a month - seven hundred and twenty a year. How much are Lemming and Orton worth? And Ellis and McKnight - that long thin man over yonder - the provision dealers? How much d'you suppose could Burges write a cheque for and not feel? 'Tisn't as if he had to save for any one now. And the same with Anstruther. I assure you we have no scruple in calling on the Visiting Brethren when we want anything. We couldn't do the work otherwise. Have you noticed how the Lodge is kept- brasswork, jewels, furniture and so on?"

"I have indeed," I said. "It's like a ship. You could eat your dinner off the floor."

"Well, come here on a by-day and you'll often find half a dozen Brethren, with eight legs between 'em, polishing and ronuking and sweeping everything they can get at. I cured a shell-shocker this spring by giving him our jewels to look after. He pretty well polished the numbers off them, but - it kept him from fighting the Huns in his sleep. And when we need Masters to take our duties - two matinees a week is rather a tax - we've the choice of P.M.'s from all over the world. The Dominions are much keener on Ritual than an average English Lodge. Besides that- Oh, we're going to adjourn. Listen to the greetings. They'll be interesting."

The crack of the great gavel brought us to our feet, after some surging and plunging among the cripples. Then the Battery Sergeant-Major, in a trained voice, delivered hearty and fraternal greetings to "Faith and Works" from his tropical District and Lodge. The others followed, without order, in every tone between a grunt and a squeak. I heard "Hauraki," "Inyan-ga-Umbezi," "Aloha," "Southern Lights" (from somewhere Puntas Arenas way), "Lodge of Rough Ashlars" (and that Newfoundland Brother looked it), two or three "Stars" of something or other, half a dozen cardinal virtues, variously arranged, hailing from Klondyke to Kalgoorlie, one Military Lodge on one of the fronts, thrown in with a severe Scots burr by my friend of the head-bandages, and the rest as mixed as the Empire itself. Just at the end there was a little stir. The silent Brother had begun to make noises; his companion tried to soothe him.

"Let him be! Let him be!" the Doctor called professionally. The man jerked and mouthed, and at last mumbled something unintelligible even to his friend, but a small, dark P.M. pushed forward importantly.

"It is all right," he said. "He wants to say," he spat out some yard-long Welsh name, adding, "That means Pembroke Docks, Worshipful Sir. We haf good Masons in Wales, too." The silent man nodded approval.

"Yes," said the Doctor, quite unmoved. "It happens that way sometimes. Hespere panta fereis, isn't it? The Star brings 'em all home. I must get
a note of that fellow's case after Lodge. I know you don't care for music," he
went on, "but I'm afraid you'll have to put up with a little more. It's a
paraphrase from Micah. Our organist arranged it. We sing it antiphonally,
as a sort of dismissal."

Even I could appreciate what followed. The singing seemed confined
to half a dozen trained voices answering each other till the last line, when
the full Lodge came in. I give it as I heard it:
"We have showed thee, O Man,
What is good.
What doth the Lord require of us?
Or Consciences' self desire of us?
But to do justly
And to love mercy
And to walk humbly with our God
As every Mason should."

Then we were played and sung out to the quaint tune of the "Entered
Apprentices' Song."

I noticed that the regular Brethren of the Lodge did not begin to take
off their regalia till the lines:
"Great Kings, Dukes and Lords
Have laid down their swords."
They moved into the anteroom, now set for the banquet, on the verse:
"Antiquity's pride
We have on our side,
Which maketh men just in their station."

The Brother (a big-boned clergyman) that I found myself next to at
table told me the custom was "a fond thing vainly invented" on the strength
of some old legend. He laid down that Masonry should be regarded as an
"intellectual abstraction." An Officer of Engineers disagreed with him, and
told us how in Flanders, a year before, some ten or twelve Brethren held
Lodge in what was left of a Church. Save for the Emblems of Mortality and
plenty of rough ashlars, there was no furniture.

"I warrant yu weren't a bit the worse for that," said the clergyman.
"The idea should be enough without trappings."

"But it wasn't," said the other. "We took a lot of trouble to make our
regalia out of camouflage-stuff that we'd pinched, and we manufactured
our jewels from old metal. I've got the set now. It kept us happy for weeks."

"Ye were absolutely irregular an' unauthorized. Whaur was your warrant?" said the Brother from the Military Lodge. "Grand Lodge ought to
take steps against —"

"If Grand Lodge had any sense," a private three places up our table
broke in, "it 'ud warrant travelling Lodges at the front and attach first-class

101

lecturers to 'em."

"Wad ye conferr degrees promiscuously?" said the scandalized Scot.

"Every time a man asked, of course. You'd have half the Army in."

The speaker played with the idea for a little while, and proved that on the lowest scale of fees Grand Lodge would get huge revenues.

"I believe," said the Engineer Officer thoughtfully, "I could design a complete travelling Lodge outfit under forty pounds weight."

"Ye're wrong. I'll prove it. We've tried ourselves," said the Military Lodge man; and they went at it together across the table, each with his own note-book.

The "banquet" was simplicity itself. Many of us ate in haste so as to get back to barracks or hospitals, but now and again a Brother came in from the outer darkness to fill a chair and empty a plate. These were Brethren who had been there before and needed no examination.

One man lurched in - helmet, Flanders mud, accoutrements and all - fresh from the leave-train.

"'Got two hours to wait for my train," he explained. "I remembered your night, though. My God, this is good!"

"What is your train and from which station?" said the clergyman, precisely. "Very well. What will you have to eat?"

"Anything. Everything. I've thrown up a month's feed off Folkestone."

He stoked himself for ten minutes without a word. Then, without a word, his face fell forward. The clergyman had him by one already limp arm and steered him to a couch, where he dropped and snored. No one took the trouble to turn round.

"Is that usual too?" I asked.

"Why not?" said the clergyman. "I'm on duty tonight to wake them for their trains. They do not respect the cloth on those occasions." He turned his broad back on me and continued his discussion with a Brother from Aberdeen by way of Mitylene where, in the intervals of mine-sweeping, he had evolved a complete theory of the Revelations of St. John the Divine in the Island of Patmos.

I fell into the hands of a Sergeant-Instructor of Machine Guns - by profession a designer of ladies' dresses. He told me that Englishwomen as a class "lose on their corsets what they make on their clothes," and that "Satan himself can't save a woman who wears thirty-shilling corsets, under a thirty-guinea costume." Here, to my grief, he was buttonholed by an earnest Lieutenant of his own branch, and became a Sergeant again all in one click.

I drifted back and forth, studying the prints on the walls I and the Masonic collections in the cases, while I listened to the inconceivable talk all round me. Little by little the company thinned, till at last there were only a dozen or so of us left. We gathered at the end of a table by the fire, the nightbird from Flanders trumpeting lustily into the hollow of his helmet, which someone bad tipped over his face.

"And how did it go with you?" said the Doctor.

"It was like a new world," I answered.

"That's what it is really." Brother Burges returned the gold pince-nez to their case and reshipped his silver spectacles. "Or that's what it might be made with a little trouble. When I think of the possibilities of he Craft at this juncture I wonder —" He stared into the fire.

"I wonder, too," said the Sergeant-Major slowly, "but - on the whole - I'm inclined to agree with you. We could do much with Masonry."

"As an aid - as an aid - not as a substitute for Religion," the clergyman snapped.

"Oh, Lord! Can't we give Religion a rest for a bit," the Doctor muttered. "It hasn't done so - I beg your pardon all round."

The clergyman was bristling. "Kamerad!" the wise Sergeant-Major went on, both hands up. "Certainly not as a substitute for a creed, but as an average plan of life. What I've seen at the front makes me sure of it."

Brother Burges came out of his muse. "There ought to be dozen - twenty - other Lodges in London every night; conferring degrees too, as well as instruction, Why shouldn't the young men join? They practice what we're always preaching. Well! Well! We must all do what we can. What's the use of old Masons if they can't give a little help along their own lines?"

"Exactly," said the Sergeant-Major, turning on the Doctor. "And what's the darn use of a Brother if he isn't allowed to help?"

"Have it your own way then," said the Doctor testily. He had evidently been approached before. He took something the Sergeant-Major handed to him and pocketed it with a nod. "I was wrong," he said to me, "when I boasted of our independence. They get round us sometimes. This," he slapped his pocket, "will give a banquet on Tuesday. We don't usually feed at matinees. It will be a surprise. By the way, try another sandwich. The ham are best." He pushed me a plate.

"They are," I said. "I've only had five or six. I've been looking for them."

"Glad you like them," said Brother Lemming. "Fed him myself, cured him myself - at my little place in Berkshire. His name was Charlemagne. By the way, Doc, am I to keep another one for next month?"

"Of course," said the Doctor, with his mouth full. "A little fatter than this chap, please. And don't forget your promise about the pickled nasturtiums. They're appreciated." Brother Lemming nodded above the pipe he had lit as we began a second supper. Suddenly the clergyman, after a glance at the clock, scooped up half a dozen sandwiches from under my nose, put them into an oiled-paper bag, and advanced cautiously towards the sleeper on the couch.

"They wake rough sometimes," said the Doctor. "Nerves, y'know." The clergyman tiptoed directly behind the man's head, and at arm's length rapped on the dome of the helmet. The man woke in one vivid streak, as the clergyman stepped back, and grabbed for a rifle that was not there.

"You've barely half an hour to catch your train." The clergyman passed him the sandwiches. "Come along."

"You're uncommonly kind and I'm very grateful," said the man, wriggling into his stiff straps. He followed his guide into the darkness after saluting.

"Who's that?" said Lemming.

"Can't say," the Doctor returned indifferently. "He's been here before. He's evidently a P.M. of sorts."

"Well! Well!" said Brother Burges, whose eyelids were drooping. "We must all do what we can. Isn't it almost time to lock up?"

"I wonder," said I, as we helped each other into our coats, "what would happen if Grand Lodge knew about all this."

"About what?" Lemming turned on me quickly.

"A Lodge of Instruction open three nights and two afternoons a week - and running a lodging-house as well. It's all very nice, but it doesn't strike me somehow as regulation."

"The point hasn't been raised yet," said Lemming. "We'll settle it after the war. Meantime we shall go on."

"There ought to be scores of them," Brother Burges repeated as we went out of the door.

"All London's full of the Craft, and no places for them to meet in. Think of the possibilities of it! Think what could have been done by Masonry through Masonry for all the world. I hope I'm not censorious, but it sometimes crosses my mind that Grand Lodge may have thrown away its chance in the war almost as much as the Church has."

"Lucky for you Brother Tamworth is taking that chap to King's Cross," said Brother Lemming, "or he'd be down your throat. What really troubles Tamworth is our legal position under Masonic Law. I think he'll inform on us one of these days. Well, good night all." The Doctor and Lemming turned off together.

"Yes," said Brother Burges, slipping his arm into mine. "Almost as much as the Church has. But perhaps I'm too much of a Ritualist."

I said nothing. I was speculating how soon I could steal a march on Brother Tamworth and inform against "Faith and Works No. 5837 E. C."

THE EGYPTIAN INFLUENCE ON OUR MASONIC CEREMONIAL AND RITUAL
by Thomas Ross

Before centering on my subject I think it would be as well if I made it quite clear that whatever antiquity may be urged for our ceremonies and ritual, our signs, words and tokens, there can be no question that shortly after the formation of the three Grand Lodges in the early part of the eighteenth century our ritual, with all that is attached to it, was much as we have it today. When I therefore enter on the object of endeavouring to prove that much of that ritual has an Egyptian origin I want the brethren to know that it was not until the year 1820, or quite 100 years after the formation of the three Grand Lodges, before there was anything like an earnest attempt made to read the hieroglyphics or sacred Writings of Egypt, while it was quite another fifty years before the Book of the Dead was deciphered and given to the world by Lepsius Wilkinson, Naville, Petrie, Wallace Budge and other enthusiastic Egyptologists.

The reading of the hieroglyphics or sacred writings was for centuries before the Christian era confined to the priests of Egypt, and was called by themselves the writing of the priests, so that when Christianity became the dominant religion in Egypt the old worship became obsolete the priests died out, and the knowledge and practice of the priestly writings went completely out of use, was neglected, forgotten, and for a period of 1500 years utterly unknown to the world.

Egyptology, or the science of studying the ancient language, history and religion from the hieroglyphics, is a thing of almost yesterday, and may be looked upon as one of the most romantic episodes in the domain of literature.

Most of you are conversant with the history of the finding of the Rosetta Stone by a French officer of artillery in 1798 in Rosetta, on the coast of Egypt. This stone is of black basalt, and is one of the most treasured relics in the Egyptian galleries in the British Museum, being the key that unlocks the mysteries of the Egyptian writings.

The Rosetta Stone is a monumental slab or tablet set up as a record of the benefactions of Ptolemy V, a king of Egypt about 195 B.C.; it contains fourteen lines of hieroglyphics, thirty-two lines of Demotic, and fifty-four of Greek, coming in that order from the top. The Greek text was easily read, a translation being published in 1801-2. Since it stated that the monument was a bilingual one (the writing of the priests and the writing of the books being the Egyptian identical with the writing of the Greeks) men of letters set themselves the task of trying to decipher the hieroglyphics.

In the years 1819 to 1822 Mr. Thomas Young, an Englishman, and M. Champollion, a Frenchman, stated that these characters, which were generally looked upon as picture-writing, were letters of an alphabetic or phonetic value. Certain characters, as may be seen in the hieroglyphic part of the stone, were written in cartouches or cartridge-shaped enclosures, and these cartouches recurred in the Greek text under the name of Ptolemy. Eventually such names as Ptolemy, Berenice and Cleopatra were spelt out, and thus a key was obtained, which enabled them to unlock the secret of reading the records of the priests of Egypt.

In the latter half of the last century Ernest Renan, the celebrated French water, truly said: "Egypt remains a lighthouse in the profound darkness of antiquity." One would almost think the compilers of our ritual had these words in mind when we read in our lectures: "The usages and customs of Freemasonry, our signs and symbols, our rites and ceremonies, correspond in a great degree with the mysteries of ancient Egypt." An assertion such as this would naturally lead one to expect in working the several degrees some reference or some allusion to the religion and mysteries of Egypt as the origin of some part at any rate of our ritual.

On the contrary however, nearly the whole of our ceremonial is attributed to episodes in the life of some member of the Jewish race as narrated in the Holy Scriptures, while almost all our words and passwords are given as being derived from the same source. Not a single one of the signs, tokens or words are pointed out as corresponding with those used in the religion or mysteries of ancient Egypt. It will be my endeavour to show the brethren wherein much of our ceremonies correspond with the religion of Egypt, and that we can fairly claim the fundamentals of the Masonic ritual to have had an origin hoary with antiquity compared with the religion of Israel.

RELIGION OF ANCIENT EGYPT

It would be as well before going further to glance briefly at the religion of Egypt, for each of the Egyptian mysteries, like those practised in Syria, Greece and Rome, was based on some circumstance in the life of their gods and goddesses.

The religion of ancient Egypt is to be found in a vast collection of religious texts, arranged in 190 chapters. They have been collected from the walls of tombs and temples, from papyrus rolls enclosed in mummy cases along with their occupants, and from writings upon the mummy cases and sarcophagi themselves. A very fine example of this being The Alabaster Sarcophagus of Seti I, who lived 1360 B. C. This very fine coffin has upon it extracts from nearly all the texts, and, many of them being illustrated, the illustrations make the text doubly interesting. The part presented to us shows the divine bark of Ra, the Sun God, being conveyed through the fourth hour of the mysteries. The bottom of the sarcophagus shows a beautiful full-size painting of the Goddess of the Heavens surrounded with texts of the same religious litany.

The name Book of the Dead has been given to these writings, and as far back as Egyptian history and traditions can go the Book of the Dead appears to have been an integral part of the religions of Egypt. No mere man was the author of this remarkable collection. The texts were dictated by God Himself at the creation of the world, to Thoth, the Scribe of the Gods, who is shown as having the body of a man and the head of a bird, and is always depicted in the act of writing the decrees of the deities. We might style Thoth the Divine emanation of wisdom and learning, the inspiration of God to man, the first to fill the place ascribed by Plato to the Divine Logos and by St. John to "The Word."

Thousands of years before Moses wrote, "In the beginning God created the heaven and the earth," the Egyptian story of the creation had been given to Egypt, where the god Nu is rising out of the primeval water bearing on his outstretched arms the boat of the sun god Ra; this is being received by the goddess of the heavens Nut, who again stands on the head of Osiris, whose body encloses the region of the underworld. In the center of the picture we have the Sacred Scarabaeus, symbol of the Creator raising himself out of the primeval void, and separating the firmament above from the waters beneath.

The *Book of the Dead* contains a history of the creation, the attributes of God, the powers and functions of the attendant gods and goddesses, as well as the ceremonies required to enable a to live such a life on earth as shall prevent his soul from being cast into that pit of fire, where the doomed one must not only suffer eternal torment, but, must undergo a species of penal servitude.

On the other hand, a man who lives a good life and acts up to the teachings of the inspired writings, will obtain from Osiris, the "Lord of Everlastingness," as his final reward, not only the crown of immortality, but a pleasant existence in the Elysian Fields. There he will live in the company of the gods, there his crops will grow luxuriantly, his cattle be sleek and docile, and there he can have the company and fellowship of those whom he loved and knew on earth. We find this belief borne out in the prayer of Sepa.

With the exception of a few tales, the records of the wars, expeditions of their rulers, detailed statements of the erection of their temples, tombs and monuments, and some hymns to the gods and goddesses, the chief and almost only literature of the Egyptians was the Book of the Dead. We can, therefore, realize how inseparably these chapters, with their formula of rubrics, litanies, ceremonies, passwords and signs must have entered into the minds and lives of the people.

To an outsider the people of Egypt almost deserved the sneer of Juvenal: "Who knows not what monsters mad Egypt can worship; whole towns worship a dog, nobody Diana"; or that of Plutarch: "The Egyptians, by adoring the animals and reverencing them as gods, have ruled their religious worship with many ridiculous rites. To this Origin, one of the Christian fathers, very pertinently replies, "Many, listening to accounts they do not understand, relative to the sacred doctrines of the Egyptian philosophers, fancy that they are acquainted with all the wisdom of Egypt, though they have never conversed with any of their priests, nor received any information from persons initiated into their mysteries."

Now, although every province, city, town, and even household had its god or trinity of gods, over and above all there reigned the Supreme Ruler of heaven and earth - the great First Cause, Creator and Preserver of all, the Great Architect of the Universe - Ra, the Sun God, called in Upper Egypt Amun Ra, "the hidden one." As proof of this, we have, in the Book of the Dead, among the many hymns to Ra, "Thou art the one God who didst come into being in the beginning of time." "Thou didst create the earth; thou didst fashion man; thou didst make the abyss of the sky; thou didst create the watery abyss; and thou didst give life to all that therein is." "O Thou One, Thou mighty One, of myriad forms and aspects." So when we contemplate the group of prominent deities in Fig. 7 we see Ra, the Great Architect in some of his myriad forms and aspects.

Ra, or Amun Ra, and the triad of Osiris, Isis and Horus were worshipped throughout the whole of Egypt from the earliest pre-dynastic times to the very end of its civilization under its native rulers, a period of anything from 7,000 to years. The worship of Isis and Horus and the ceremonial of Ra and Osiris have survived to the present day, though under different names; the former in a branch of the Christian Church, and the latter, as I hope to show, in our Masonic cult.

Having set forth this general claim for the close connection between our ancient moral system and that of Egypt, let me show briefly under separate headings how some of our more familiar symbols, traditions and ceremonies may be explained in the light of Egyptology.

THE POINT WITHIN A CIRCLE

The God Ra is written phonetically with the hieroglyphs R. and A., i.e., a mouth and an arm, followed by the two ideographs, a circle with a dot in the centre and a seated god. But on most occasions the name of Ra, the Sun God, is written with the ideograph of a point within a circle, as though the name was of "too essential a nature to be fully comprehended by human wisdom or clearly pronounced by the tongue of any individual."

This sign of a point within a circle was used by the kings of Egypt for thousands of years as their royal title to the throne, while they did not scruple to style themselves, sons of Ra. The same sign is even today used by astronomers in writing of the sun as the centre of the heavenly bodies, and is referred to in our Masonic ritual.

MASTER AND WARDENS

The sun, being the visible emblem of the god Ra, had three names or aspects. In the morning he was Kheper Ra, or Ra Harmachis, the opener of the day. The Sphinx, the oldest monument in the world, was called Ra Harmachis, the rising sun. This huge figure, with the face and head of a man and the body of a lion, is 140 feet long and over 60 feet in height. As it sits there facing "the east, to open and enliven the glorious day," it represents wisdom and strength. For thousands of years also it represented beauty, for in 1200 A. D. the learned Arab, Abd-el-Latif, described the face as being very beautiful and the mouth as graceful and lovely.

At midday, when the sun was at his meridian, he was Ra, the strong one: "When all beasts and cattle reposed in their pastures and the trees and green herbs put forth their leaves."

At even he was Atmu, or Temu, the closer of the day: "When thou settest in the western horizon the earth is in darkness and is like a being that is dead." This last quotation is strikingly shown in the illustration to chap. xviii. of the *Book of the Dead*. The Sun God, in shape of the Sacred Eagle with disc on head and folded wings, is about to set in the mountains of the west. Isis and Nepthys, sister goddesses, are adoring two lions, representing the sun of yesterday and the sun of tomorrow - a fine allegory of past, present and future.

Thus we see that Ra Harmachis, like our W.M. was placed in the east; Ra, like our J. W., represented the sun at its meridian; and Temu, like our S. W., is placed in the west to close the day, or, as the Egyptian ritual puts it: "I am Ra Harmachis in the morning, Ra in his noontide, Temu in the evening."

THE. TWO GREAT PILLARS

Next in importance to the worship of Ra, the Sun God, was the cult of Osiris and Isis and of Isis and Horus. The adoration of these gods and this goddess was not only the dominant religion in Egypt from the very earliest until the latest times, but during nearly a thousand years it had spread into Phoenicia, Greece, Rome, and throughout the whole of the Roman Empire. In many cases Osiris is identified with Ra, the Sun God, while Isis is most frequently shown wearing the disc of the moon or the crescent moon on her head.

In the texts Isis is the divine consort of Ra Osiris. She is the moon who rules the night as the sun rules the day; and every month at Now Moon she gathered the sun into her lap to be impregnated anew. "That I may behold the face of the sun and that I may behold the moon for ever and ever," was the great wish of the pious Egyptian (*Book of the Dead*, chap. xviii).

Osiris and Isis are often pictured as the two eyes of Ra, and in that capacity enter largely into the mysteries of Ra. Now, when we consider how much the sun and moon bulked in the worship of the Egyptians and surrounding nations, let us see what effect this would be likely to have on those two great pillars placed by King Solomon at the porchway or entrance to his temple at Jerusalem. Before the temple of the sun at Heliopolis (the On of Genesis), Osertsen the First (of the twelfth dynasty B. C. 2435) set up two obelisks. One of them remains there today, the only trace left of that gorgeous building where Joseph's father-in-law served as priest to the Sun God, where Moses, as the adopted son of Pharaoh, must have worshipped and conducted the mysteries of the temple; and where, two thousand years later, learned Grecians like Herodotus came to study. These two obelisks would undoubtedly represent the two most important objects in the worship of the heavenly bodies, the sun and the moon, Osiris Ra and Isis.

About 1000 years later, or, to be exact, B.C. 1566, Queen Hatasoo, of the eighteenth dynasty, set up two obelisks in front of the Temple of the Sun at Karnak. They are there today, the one standing, the other fallen down, a memorial to the worship of the two heavenly bodies.

I have a work published in 1757, "Travels in Egypt, by Frederick Lewis Norden, Capt Danish Navy." Captain Norden visited Karnak on 11th December, 1737. In his book he has plates in the old copper engraving, and among them he has a wonderful view, which I have copied from his book. Speaking of this plate, he says: "I drew magnificent antiquities in all the situations is was possible for me and as they offered themselves to my sight."

We can see by Captain Norden's drawing that obelisks were standing at the entrance to the temple less than two hundred years ago. So that the artist who made for us the drawing of Karnak restored, placed the obelisks in the position they originally stood when set up by Queen Hatasoo nearly 3600 years ago. The queen, in an inscription on the walls of her temple, describes them as "two great obelisks of granite of the south, and the summit of each is covered with copper and gold, the very best which can be obtained; they shall be seen from untold distances, and they shall flood the land with their rays of light. I have done these things because of the loving heart I possess towards my father, Amun Ra, the Sun God."

Some centuries later at Medinet Abu was placed a very fine pair of pillars at the porchway or entrance to the temple. We see by this that the obelisk has given place to a pillar with an ornamental capital. These pillars were set up by Rameses III about 1200 B.C., or quite 200 years before King Solomon built the Holy Temple at Jerusalem.

The pillar seems to have been largely used in the religious thinking of the Egyptians, either as an emblem of the Deity or a thank-offering from the worshippers. In many of the temples to-day there are beautiful lotus and papyrus pillars, while in numerous vignettes in the Book of the Dead we have Osiris seated in a shrine upheld by two graceful pillars. Now, when we see that not only in Egypt, but in the surrounding countries, the worship of the sun and the moon was not only the prevailing but the popular religion of the people, there is little to be wondered at that when the Israelites left Egypt they not only carried away with them a very strong bias in favor of this worship, but had that propensity considerably strengthened when they settled down among the sun and moon worshippers of Palestine. So rampant was this prejudice in flavor of sun and moon worship, that we find Moses denouncing it in no unmeasured terms, and threatening death on the "man or woman that hath brought wickedness in the sight of the Lord thy God in transgressing His covenant, and hath gone and served other gods and worshipped them, either the sun or the moon" (Deut. xvii. 2, 3). In spite of these warnings, however we find years afterwards "Josiah put down the idolatrous priests, whom the kings of Judah had ordained to burn incense to the sun and to the moon" (2 Kings xxiii. 5). Again we read, "At that time, saith the lord, they shall bring out the bones of the brings of Judah, and the bones of his Princes, and the bones of the inhabitants of Jerusalem out of their graves, and they shall spread them before the sun and the moon whom they have loved and whom they have worshipped" (Jer. viii. 1, 2).

Ezekiel saw "five and twenty men with their backs towards the temple of the Lord and their faces towards the east, and they worshipped the sun towards the east" (Ezek. viii. 16). The Jewish women told Jeremiah: "But we will certainly do whatsoever thing goeth forth out of our own mouth to burn incense unto the Queen of Heaven (the moon or Isis) and to pour out drink unto her as we have done, we and our fathers and our kings and our princes in the cities of Judah and in the streets of Jerusalem" (Jer. xlix. 17). One more quotation, this time from the sorely afflicted Man of Uz: "If I beheld the sun when it shines or the moon walking in brightness, and my heart hath been secretly enticed or my mouth hath kissed my hand" (Job xxxi. 26, 27).

When we thus see the influence that sun and moon worship had upon the children of the Exodus, and when we consider that though settled in Palestine they were surrounded by nations who paid homage to the sun and moon under the names of Osiris Ra and Isis, Baal and Astarte, Milcom and Ashtoreth, and Adonis and Cybele, and when we read that Solomon took to himself wives from Egypt, Moab, Ammon, Edmon and Phoenicia we are quite prepared for the information given in I Kings xi. 5 that "Solomon went after Ashtoreth, the Goddess of the Zidonians (the moon), and after Milcom, the abomination of the Ammonites (the sun)."

This brings us to still another consideration that, in view of these telling quotations from Scripture, are we not justified in assuming when Solomon put up those two great pillars at the porchway or entrance to the temple they had an esoteric meaning entirely different from that ascribed to them in holy writ and that only by adopting the view I shall now put before you as to the signification of those pillars can we bring in the meaning given to them in our ritual.

We are told that the pillar on the left denoted strength, while that on the right signified to establish. Let us suppose that these two pillars, no matter by what names they were called, had also a hidden meaning, what more appropriate conception for signifying strength could be selected than the Sun God. The sun was all powerful, all beneficent, daily observing all that transpired on earth, while the pillar on the right, if we put it down as representing the moon goddess, would answer as the Establisher. The phases of the moon marked out the weeks, each moon was a lunar month, and with unfailing regularity she indicated the Jewish festivals, marking them to stand firm forever, and when conjoined with the strength of the sun what better designation could be applied than stability?

If we consider the question carefully and reflect on all that the sun and the moon stood for to these people at this particular time, we can see that strength and stability would be a more apt interpretation for those bodies than could be deduced from the great-grandfather of David and the assistant high priest at the dedication of the temple. Reading certain passages of the Psalms helps to confirm us in this. "They shall fear Thee as long as the sun and moon endure throughout all generations." (Ps. lxxii. 5.) "It shall be established forever as the moon." (Ps.lxxxix. 37). "He appointed the moon for seasons, the sun knoweth his going down." (Ps. civ. 19).

Another shown is from an ancient Cyprian coin depicting the old temple of Aphrodite, at Paphos, built about 100 years before the temple at Jerusalem. In addition to the pillars at each side of the entrance to the temple, the sun and moon are also represented as adorning the top of the building. Let us bear in mind that Solomon's intimate friend and adviser was Hiram, King of Tyre, that his Chief Master Mason was Hiram Abif, that his principal architect was Adoniram, all Phoenicians; that this temple of Paphos, which was at the time the glory of the Mediterranean Coast and lay only a short distance from Tyre, would powerfully influence the minds of these in the immediate vicinity. Nor is it improbable that the architecture of this temple, with its pillars, would appeal to the Phoenician craftsmen and would largely guide them in suggesting to Solomon a similar style of sanctuary in the house he was about to build for the Lord God of Israel. There is yet another motive that may have influenced Solomon in dedicating these pillars to solar deities. Professor Sayee says that Hadad was the Supreme Baal or sun god of Babylonia and that his worship was widespread in Palestine and Syria, also that the abbreviated form of the name of Hadad was Dad, Dadu, and the biblical David. If therefore David was the Palestinian name for Baal, the sun god, what more likely than that Solomon would be ready to take this opportunity of perpetuating the memory of his illustrious father.

The *Encyclopedia Biblica*, in treating of the two pillars, suggests that the names given are enigmatical and that they must have a religious significance. That not improbably the full name of the pillar on the left hand is Baal-zebul (dwelling of the sun), and in later times probably the name of the second pillar was literately mutilated because of the new and inauspicious associations which had gathered round it. Solomon, to have been consistent with the teachings of Moses, should have erected only one pillar as a symbol of that unity of the Divine Being, which was so integral a part of the worship of the Israelites.

In setting up two pillars he was conforming to the belief of every one of the surrounding nations, i.e., A duality in the divine, the sun and moon representing the active and passive principle in nature, the male and female element. Coming down to later times we find these two pillars prominent in Druidic enclosures used for the rites of sun worship, while the two steeples or towers at the front of our Christian cathedrals and churches look as if they were an unconscious survival of the votive obelisks or pillars erected to the sun or moon before the temples of Egypt.

ANDERSON'S CONSTITUTIONS OF 1723
by Lionel Vibert

The Grand Lodge that was brought into existence in 1717 did not find it necessary to possess a Constitution of its own for some years. Exactly what went on between 1717 and 1721 we do not know; almost our only authority being the account given by Anderson in 1738 which is unreliable in many particulars. Indeed it cannot be stated with certainty whether there were any more than the original Four Old Lodges until 1721; it would appear from the Lists and other records we possess that the first lodge to join them did not do so till July of that year; the statements as to the number of new lodges in each year given by Anderson are not capable of verification. It was also in the year 1721 that the Duke of Montagu was made Grand Master on 24th June, having probably joined the Craft just previously. The effect of his becoming Grand Master, a fact advertised in the dally press of the period, was that the Craft leapt into popularity, its numbers increased, and new lodges were rapidly constituted. Even now it was not anticipated that the Grand Lodge would extend the scope of its activities beyond London and Westminster, but Grand Master Payne, possibly anticipating the stimulus that would be provided by the accession to the Craft of the Duke, had got ready a set of General Regulations, and these were read over on the occasion of his installation. Unfortunately we do not possess the original text of them but have only the version as revised and expanded by Anderson. But we can understand that in a very short time it would be found necessary for these regulations to be printed and published to the Craft. Their publication was undertaken by Anderson, who took the opportunity to write a history of the Craft as an introduction, and to prepare a set of Charges; his intention clearly being to give the new body a work which would in every respect replace the Old Manuscript Constitutions. The work consists of a dedication written by Desaguliers and addressed to Montagu as late Grand Master; a Historical introduction; a set of six Charges; Payne's Regulations revised; the manner of constituting a new lodge; and songs for the Master, Wardens, Fellow Craft and Entered Apprentice, of which the last is well known in this country (England) and is still sung today in many lodges. There is also an elaborate frontispiece. The work was published by J. Senex and J. Hooke, on 28th February, 1722-3, that is to say 1722 according to the official or civil reckoning, but 1723 by the so-called New Style, the popular way of reckoning. (It did not become the official style till the reform of the calender in 1752.) The title page bears the date 1723 simply.

Dr. Anderson was born in Aberdeen, and was a Master of Arts of the Marischal College in that city. He was in London in 1710 and was minister of a Presbyterian Chapel in Swallow Street, Piccaldilly, till 1734. He was also chaplain to the Earl of Buchan, and as the Earl was a representative peer for Scotland from 1714-1734, it was probably during these years that he maintained a London establishment. We do not know that the Earl was a Mason, although his sons were. When Anderson was initiated we do not know either; but it may have been in the Aberdeen Lodge. There is a re-markable similarity between his entry in the Constitutions of his name as "Master of a Lodge and Author of this Book," and in entry in the Aberdeen Mark Book, of "James Anderson, Glazier and Mason and Writer of this Book." This was in 1670 and this James Anderson is no doubt another per-son. It just happens most unfortunately that the minutes for the precise period during which we might expect to find our author are missing. In any case he was familiar with the Scottish terminology which he no doubt had some share in introducing into English Freemasonry.

Nor can it be stated with confidence when he joined the Craft in Lon-don. He was Master of a lodge in 1722, a lodge not as yet identified, but there is no record of his having had anything to do with Grand Lodge prior to the Grand Mastership of the Duke of Montagu. He was not even present at the Duke's installation; at all events Stukeley does not name him as being there. He himself, in his version of the minutes, introduces his own name for the first time at the next meeting.

HOW HE CAME TO WRITE THE WORK

His own account of the work, as given in 1738, is that he was ordered to digest the Old Gothic Constitutions in a new and better method by Montagu on 29th September, 1721, that on 27th December, Montagu ap-pointed fourteen learned brothers to examine the MS., and that after they had approved it was ordered to be printed on 25th March, 1722. He goes on to say that it was produced in print for the approval of Grand Lodge on 17th January, 1722-3, when Grand Master Wharton's manner of constituting a lodge was added. In the book itself are printed a formal Approbation by Grand Lodge and the Masters and Wardens of twenty lodges (with the ex-ception of two Masters), which is undated, and also a copy of a resolution of the Quarterly Communication of 17th January, 1722-3, directing the publi-cation and recommending it to the Craft.

With regard to the committee of fourteen learned brethren and the three occasions on which the book is alleged to have been considered in Grand Lodge, the Approbation itself states that the author first submitted his text for the perusal of the late and present Deputy Grand Master's and of other learned brethren and also the Masters of lodges, and then delivered it to

Grand Master Montagu, who by the advice of several brethren ordered the same to be handsomely printed, This is not quite the same thing.

And it is to be noted that in 1735 Anderson appeared before Grand Lodge to protest against the doings of one Smith who had pirated the Constitutions which were his sole property. His account of this incident in the 1738 edition suppresses this interesting circumstance. Further it is very clear from the Grand Lodge minutes that the appearance of the book caused a good deal of dissension in Grand Lodge itself, and it brought the Craft into ridicule from outside; in particular Anderson's re-writing of Payne's Regulations was taken exception to. Anderson himself did not appear again in Grand Lodge for nearly eight years.

The true state of the case appears to be that Anderson undertook to write the work as a private venture of his own and that this was sanctioned, since it was desirable that the Regulations at least published, without any very careful examination of his text, or of so much of it as was ready, and that when it was published it was discovered, but too late, that he had taken what were felt by many to be unwarrantable liberties not only with the traditional Charges but also with Payne's Regulations.

THE BOOK IS ANALYZED

In using the term Constitutions he was following the phraseology of several of the versions of the Old Charges, and in fact the word occurs (in Latin) in the Regius, though Anderson never saw that. It was apparently traditional in the Craft. The contents of the work itself indicate that the various portions were put together at different dates and Anderson tells us it was not all in print during Montagu's term of office.

Taking the Approbation first, this is signed by officers of twenty lodges; the Master and both Wardens have all signed in all but two. In those, numbers eight and ten, the place for the Master's signature is blank. Mr. Mathew Birkhead is shown as Master of number five; and he died on the 30th December, 1722. Accordingly the Approbation must be of an earlier date and of the twenty lodges we know that number nineteen was constituted on 25th November, 1722, and number twenty if, as is probable, it is of later date, will have been constituted possibly on the same day but more probably a few days later. Thus we can date the Approbation within narrow limits. In his 1738 edition Anderson gives a series of the numbers of lodges on the roll of Grand Lodge at different dates which cannot be checked from any independent source, and he suggests that on 25th March, 1722, there were already at least twenty-four lodges in existence because he asserts that representatives of twenty-four paid their homage to the Grand Master on that date; and that those of twenty-five did so on 17th January, 1722-3. Because of Anderson's assertion as to twenty-four lodges some writers have speculated as to the lodges the officers of which omitted to sign or which were ignored by the author. But the truth probably is that these lodges - if they existed at all - were simply not represented at the meeting.

The Approbation is signed by Wharton as Grand Master, Desaguliers as Deputy, and Timson and Hawkins as Grand Wardens. According to the story as told by Anderson in 1738 Wharton got himself elected Grand Master irregularly on 24th June, 1722, when he appointed these brethren as his Wardens but omitted to appoint a Deputy. On 17th January, 1722-3, the Duke of Montagu, "to heal the breach," had Wharton proclaimed Grand Master and he then appointed Desaguliers as his Deputy and Timson and Anderson, (not Hawkins,) Wardens and Anderson adds that his appointment was made for Hawkins demitted as always out of town. If this story could be accepted the Approbation was signed by three officers who were never in office simultaneously, since when Desaguliers came in Hawkins had already demitted. This by itself would throw no small doubt on Anderson's later narrative, but in fact we know that his whole story as to Wharton is a tissue of fabrication. The daily papers of the period prove that the Duke of Wharton was in fact installed on 25th June, and he then appointed Desaguliers as his Deputy and Timson and Hawkins as his Wardens. It is unfortunate that Anderson overlooked that his very date, 24th June, was impossible as it was a Sunday, a day expressly prohibited by Payne's Regulations for meetings of Grand Lodge. There are indications of some disagreement; apparently some brethren wished Montagu to continue, but in fact Wharton went in the regular course; the list of Grand Lodge officers in the minute book of Grand Lodge shows him as Grand Master in 1722.

And that Hawkins demitted is merely Anderson's allegation. In this same list he appears as Grand Warden, but Anderson himself has written the words (which he is careful to reproduce in 1738): "Who demitted and James Anderson A.M. was chosen in his place;" vide the photographic reproduction of the entry at page 196 of Quatuor, Coronatorum Antigrapha Vol. X; while in the very first recorded minute of Grand Lodge, that of 24th June, 1723, the entry as to Grand Wardens originally stood: Joshua Timson and the Reverend Mr. James Anderson who officiated for Mr. William Hawkins. But these last six words have been carefully erased, vide the photo reproduction at page 48 *Quatuor Corontorum Antigrapha* VOL X, which brings them to light again. Hawkins then was still the Grand Warden in June 1723, and on that occasion Anderson officiated for him at the January meeting. The explanation of the whole business appears to be that Anderson in 1738 was not anxious to emphasize his associated with Wharton, who after his term of office as Grand Master proved a renegade and Jacobite and an enemy to the Craft. He had died in Spain in 1731. For the Book of Constitutions of 1738 there is a new Approbation altogether.

But we have not yet done with this Approbation for the further question arises, At what meeting of Grand Lodge was it drawn up? The license to publish refers to a meeting of 17th January, 1722-23, and that there was such a meeting is implied by the reference to this document in the official minutes of June, when the accuracy of this part of it is not impugned. But this Approbation was as we have seen drawn up between the end of November and the end of December, 1722, and between these limits an earlier date, is more probable than a later. No such meeting is mentioned by Anderson himself in 1738. But the explanation of this no doubt is that he now has his tale of the proclamation of Wharton at that meeting on 17th January, and any references to a meeting of a month or so earlier presided over by that nobleman would stultify the narrative. It is probable that a meeting was in fact held, and that its occurrence was suppressed by Anderson when he came to publish his narrative of the doings of Grand Lodge fifteen years later. The alternative would be that the whole document was unauthorized, but so impudent an imposture could never have escaped contemporary criticism. Truly the ways of the deceiver are hard.

THE FRONTISPIECE IS DESCRIBED

The Frontispiece to the Constitutions of 1723, which was used over again without alteration in 1738, represents a classical arcade in the foreground of which stand two noble personages, each attended by three others of whom one of those on the spectator's left carries cloaks and pairs of gloves. The principal personages can hardly be intended for any others than Montagu and Wharton; and Montagu is wearing the robes of the Garter, and is handing his successor a roll of the Constitutions, not a book. This may be intended for Anderson's as yet unprinted manuscript, or, more likely it indicates that a version of the Old Constitutions was regarded at the time as part of the Grand Master's equipment, which would be a survival of Operative practice. Behind each Grand Master stand their officers, Beal, Villeneau, and Morris on one side, and on the other Desaguliers, Timson, and Hawkins, Desaguliers as a clergyman and the other two in ordinary dress, and evidently an attempt has been made in each case to give actual portraits. It is unnecessary to suppose, as we would have to if we accepted Anderson's story, that this plate was designed, drawn, and printed in the short interval between 17th January and 28th February. It might obviously have been prepared at any time after June 25, 1722. By it Anderson is once more contradicted, because here is Hawkins - or at all events someone in ordinary clothes - as Grand Warden, and not the Reverend James Anderson, as should be the case if Wharton was not Grand Master till January and then replaced the absent Hawkins by the Doctor. The only other plate in the book is an elaborate illustration of the arms of the Duke of Montagu which stands at the head of the first page of the dedication.

We can date the historical portion of the work from the circumstance that it ends with the words: "our present worthy Grand Master, the most noble Prince John, Duke of Montagu." We can be fairly certain that

Anderson's emendations of Payne's Regulations were in part made after the incidents of Wharton's election because they contain elaborate provisions for the possible continuance of the Grand Master and the nomination or election of his successor and in the charges again, there is a reference to the Regulations hereunto annexed. But beyond this internal evidence, (and that of the Approbation and sanction to publish already referred to), the only guide we have to the dates of printing the various sections of the work is the manner in which the printers' catch words occur. The absence of a catch word is not proof that the sections were printed at different times because it might be omitted if, e. g., it would spoil the appearance of a tail-piece; but the occurrence of a catch word is a very strong indication that the sections it links were printed together. Now in the Constitution of 1723 they occur as follows: from the dedication to the history, none; from the history to the Charges, catch word; from the Charges to a Postscript 'put in here to fill a page', catch word; from this to the Regulations, none; from the Regulations to the method of constituting a New Lodge, catch word; from this to the Approbation, none; from the Approbation to the final section, the songs, none; and none from here to the license to publish on the last page.

Accordingly we may now date the several portions of the work with some degree of certainty. The times are as follows:

The plate; at any time after June 25th, 1722.

The dedication, id., but probably written immediately before publication.

The historical portion; prior to 25th June, 1722.

The charges printed with the preceding section, but drafted conjointly with the Regulations.

The postscript; the same.

The General Regulations, after Wharton's installation

The method of constituting a new Lodge; printed with the preceding section.

The Approbation; between 25th November and end of December, 1722.

The songs and sanction to publish; after January 17th, 1722-3, and probably at the last moment.

Of these sections the plate and Approbation have already been dealt with. The dedication calls for no special notice; it is an extravagant eulogy of the accuracy and diligence of the author. The songs are of little interest except the familiar Apprentice's Song, and this is now described as by our late Brother Matthew Birkhead.

THE HISTORICAL PORTION

This requires a somewhat extended notice. The legendary history, as it is perhaps not necessary to remind my readers, brought Masonry or Geometry from the children of Lamech to Solomon; then jumped to France and

Charles Martel; and then by St. Alban, Athelstan and Edwin, this worthy Craft was established in England. In the Spencer family of MSS. an attempt has been made to fill in the obvious gaps in this narrative by introducing the second and third temples, those of Zerubbabel and Herod, and Auviragus king of Britain as a link with Rome, France and Charles Martel being dropped, while a series of monarchs has also been introduced between St. Alban's paynim king and Atheistan. Anderson's design was wholly different. He was obsessed by the idea of the perfection of the Roman architecture, what he called the Augustan Style, and he took the attitude that the then recent introduction of Renaissance architecture into England as a return to a model from which Gothic had been merely a barbarous lapse. He traces the Art from Cain who built a city, and who was instructed in Geometry by Adam. Here he is no doubt merely bettering his originals which were content with the sons of Lamech. The assertion shows a total want of any sense of humor, but then so do all his contributions to history. But it is worth while pointing out that it suggests more than this; it suggests that he had an entire lack of acquaintance with the polite literature of the period. No well-read person of the day would be unacquainted with the writings of Abraham Cowley, the poet and essayist of the Restoration, and the opening sentence of his Essay of Agriculture is: "The three first men in the world were a gardener, a ploughman and a grazier; and if any man object that the second of these was a murderer, I desire he would consider that as soon as he was so he quitted our profession, and turned builder." It is difficult to imagine that Anderson would have claimed Cain as the first Mason if he had been familiar with this passage.

From this point he develops the history in his own fashion, but he incorporates freely and with an entire disregard for textual accuracy any passages in the Old Charges that suit him and he has actually used the Cooke Text, as also some text closely allied to the William Watson. We know the Cooke was available to him; we learn from Stukeley that it had been produced in Grand Lodge on 24 June, 1721. Anderson, in 1738, omits all reference to this incident, but asserts that in 1718 Payne desired the brethren to bring to Grand Lodge any old writings and records, and that several copies of the Gothic Constitutions (as he calls them) were produced and collated. He also alleges that in 1720 several valuable manuscripts concerning the Craft were too hastily burnt by some scrupulous brethren. The former of these statements we should receive with caution; for the very reason that the 1723 Constitutions show no traces of such texts; the latter may be true and the manuscripts may have been rituals, or they may have been versions of the Old Charges, but there was nothing secret about those. The antiquary Plot had already printed long extracts from them.

Returning to the narrative we are told that Noah and his sons were Masons, which is a statement for which Anderson found no warrant in his originals; but he seems to have had a peculiar fondness for Noah. In 1738 he speaks of Masons as true Noachidae, alleging this to have been their first name according to some old traditions, and it is interesting to observe that the Irish Constitutions of 1858 preserve this fragment of scholarship and assert as a fact that Noachidae was the first name of Masons. Anderson also speaks of the three great articles of Noah, which are not however further elucidated, but it is probable that the reference is to the familiar triad of Brotherly Love, Relief and Truth. He omits Abraham and introduces Euclid in his proper chronological sequence, so that he has corrected the old histories to that extent; but after Solomon and the second Temple he goes to Greece, Sicily and Rome, where was perfected the glorious Augustan Style. He introduces Charles Martel - as King of France! - as helping England to recover the true art after the Saxon invasion, but ignores Athelstan and Edwin.

He however introduces most of the monarchs after the Conquest and makes a very special reference to Scotland and the Stuarts. In the concluding passage he used the phrase "the whole body resembles a well built Arch" and it has been suggested, not very convincingly perhaps, that this is an allusion to the Royal Arch Degree.

There is an elaborate account of Zerubbabel's temple which may have some such significance, and the Tabernacle of Moses, Aholiab and Bezaleel is also mentioned at some length, Moses indeed being a Grand Master. He also inserts for no apparent reason a long note on the words Hiram Abiff, and in this case the suggestion that there is a motive for his doing so connected with ritual is of more cogency. It is an obvious suggestion that the name was of importance to the Craft at this date, that is to say early in 1722, and that the correctness of treating Abiff as a surname instead of as equivalent to his "father" was a matter the Craft were taking an interest in.

THE SIX CHARGES

The Charges, of which there are six, are alleged to be extracted from ancient records of lodges beyond Sea, and of those in England, Scotland and Ireland. In the Approbation the assertion is that he has examined several copies from Italy and Scotland and sundry parts of England. Were it not that he now omits Ireland altogether we might nave been disposed to attach some importance to the former statement. As yet no Irish version of the Old Charges has come to light but it is barely possible that there were records of Irish Freemasonry at the time which have since passed out of sight, a Freemasonry no doubt derived originally from England. But the discrepancy is fatal; we must conclude that the worthy doctor never saw any Irish record. And we can safely dismiss his lodges in Italy or beyond Sea as equally mythical.

Of the six Charges themselves the first caused trouble immediately on its appearance. It replaced the old invocation of the Trinity and whatever else there may have been of statements of religious and Christian belief in the practice of the lodges by a vague statement that we are only to be obliged to that religion in which all men agree. Complete religious tolerance has in fact become the rule of our Craft, but the Grand Lodge of 1723 was not ready for so sudden a change and it caused much ill feeling and possibly many secessions. It was the basis of a series of attacks on the new Grand Lodge.

CONSTITUTING A NEW LODGE

The manner of constituting a New Lodge is noteworthy for its reference to the "Charges of a Master," and the question, familiar to us today: Do you submit to these charges as Masters have done in all ages? It does not appear that these are the six ancient Charges of a previous section; they were something quite distinct. But not until 1777 are any Charges of the Master known to have been printed. It is also worthy of notice that the officers to be appointed Wardens of the new lodge are Fellow Crafts. There is also a reference to the Charges to the Wardens which are to be given by a Grand Warden. This section appeared in the Constitutions of the United Grand Lodge as late as 1873.

Anderson in 1738 alleges that he was directed to add this section to the work at the meeting of January 17 and he then speaks of it as the ancient manner of constituting a lodge. This is also the title of the corresponding section in the 1738 Constitutions, which is only this enlarged. But its title in 1723 is: Here follows the Manner of constituting a NEW LODGE, as practised by His Grace the Duke of Wharton, the present Right Worshipful Grand Master, according to the ancient Usages of Masons. We once more see Anderson suppressing references to the Duke of Wharton where he can in 1738, and yet obliged to assert that the section was added after January 17th in order to be consistent in his story. It is not in the least likely that this is what was done. It was to all appearance printed at one and the same time with the Regulations, which he himself tells us were in print on 17th January, and since Wharton constituted four lodges if not more in 1722 he will not have waited six months to settle his method. We may be pretty certain that this section was in print before the Approbation to which it is not linked by a catch-word.

THE REGULATIONS

The Regulations, as I have already mentioned, have come down to us only as rewritten by Anderson. The official minutes of Grand Lodge throw considerable light on the matter. The first of all relates to the appointment of the Secretary, and the very next one is as follows:

The Order of the 17th January 1722-3 printed at the end of the Constitutions page 91 for the publishing the said Constitutions as read purporting, that they had been before approved in Manuscript by the Grand Lodge and were then (viz) 17th January aforesaid produced in print and approved by the Society.

Then the Question was moved, that the said General Regulations be confirmed, so far as they are consistent with the Ancient Rules of Masonry. The previous question was moved and put, whether the words "so far as they are consistent with the Ancient Rules of Masonry" be part of the Question. Resolved in the affirmative, But the main Question was not put.

And the Question was moved that it is not in the Power of any person, or Body of men, to make any alteration, or Innovation in the Body of Masonry without the consent first obtained of the Annual Grand Lodge. And the Question being put accordingly Resolved in the Affirmative.

We would record these proceedings today in somewhat different form, perhaps as follows:

It was proposed (and seconded) that the said General Regulations be confirmed so far as they are consistent with the Ancient Rules of Masonry. An amendment to omit the words "so far ... Masonry" was negatived. But in place of the original proposition the following resolution was adopted by a majority: That it is not, etc.

The effect of this is that it indicates pretty clearly that there was a strong feeling in Grand Lodge that Anderson's version of the Regulations had never been confirmed; that there was a difference of opinion as to now confirming them, even partially; and that in fact this was not done, but a resolution was adopted instead condemning alterations made without the consent of Grand Lodge at its annual meeting first obtained. I should perhaps say that the word "purporting" does not here have the meaning we would today attach to it; it has no sense of misrepresentation. Anderson was present at this meeting, but naturally not a word of all this appears in the account he gives of it in 1738.

Regulation XIII, or one sentence in it rather, "Apprentices must be admitted Masters and Fellow Craft only here, (i.e. in Grand Lodge) unless by a Dispensation," was at one time the battle ground of the Two Degree versus Three Degree schools; but it is generally admitted now, I believe, that only two degrees are referred to, namely the admission and the Master's Part.

The order of the words is significant. In the Regulation they read "Masters and Fellow Craft." In the resolution of 27 November, 1725 by which the rule was annulled, the wording is "Master" in the official minutes, which is a strong indication that the original Regulation only referred to one degree. In 1738 Anderson deliberately alters what is set out as the original wording and makes it read "Fellow Crafts and Masters," while in the new Regulation printed alongside of it the alteration of 27 November, 1725, is quoted as

"Masters and Fellows" both being inaccurate; and he even gives the date wrongly.

The second Regulation enacts that the Master of a particular lodge has the right of congregating the members of his lodge into a chapter upon any emergency as well as to appoint the time and place of their usual forming. But it would be quite unsafe to assume that this is another reference to the Royal Arch; it appears to deal with what we would now call an emergent meeting.

Payne's, or rather Anderson's, Regulations were the foundation on which the law of the Craft was based, it being developed by a continual process of emendation and addition, and their phraseology can still be traced in our English Constitutions today.

SUBSEQUENT ALTERATIONS

In America Franklin reprinted this work in 1734 apparently verbatim. In 1738 Anderson brought out a second addition which was intended to replace the earlier one altogether, but it was a slovenly performance and the Regulations were printed in so confused a manner, being all mixed up with notes and amendments (many inaccurately stated), that it was difficult to make head or tail of them and to ascertain what was the law of the Craft. He also re-wrote the history entirely and greatly expanded it, introducing so many absurdities that Gould has suggested that he was deliberately fooling the Grand Lodge, or in the alternative that he was himself in his dotage. He died very shortly after. But this same ridiculous history has done duty in all seriousness till comparatively recent years, being brought up to date by Preston and others who were apparently quite unconscious of its true value. Unfortunately that portion of the history which professed to give an account of the proceedings of Grand Lodge and for which the official minutes were at Anderson's disposal is full of what one must consider wilful inaccuracies and misstatements.

In the next edition of the Constitutions, 1754, the Regulations were re-written by Entick, but the history was preserved. Entick also reverted to the Charges as drawn up in 1723 into which, especially the first, Anderson had introduced various modifications in 1738, and those Charges are the basis of the Ancient Charges to be found today in the Constitutions of the United Grand Lodge of England, the only differences, except as regards the first Charge, not amounting to more than verbal modifications.

OUR DEBT TO ANDERSON

While as students we are bound to receive any statement that Anderson makes with the utmost caution unless it can be tested from other sources, we must not be too ready to abuse the worthy Doctor on that account. Our standards of historical and literary accuracy are higher than those of 1723, and his object was to glorify Montagu and the Craft and the new style of architecture introduced by Inigo Jones and others of his school; and this he did wholeheartedly, and if in the process he twisted a text or two or supplied suitable events to fill gaps in his narrative for which mere history as such had failed to record facts, no one at the time would think any the worse of him for that. It was a far more serious matter that he was instrumental in removing from the literature of the Craft all definite religious allusions; but as we now see, the Craft in fact owes its universality today to its wide undenominationalism and in this respect he built better than he knew. The Constitutions of 1723 remains one of our most important texts and only awaits publication in full facsimile with suitable notes and introduction at the hands of some Society with the requisite funds.

THE RISE AND DEVELOPMENT OF
ANTI-MASONRY IN AMERICA, 1737-1826
by J. Hugo Tatsch

Anti-Masonry appeared in America very soon after the revitalized fraternity of England made its influence felt in the American colonies. Only twenty years after the Revival of 1717 took place in England, and within a decade after the first positive traces of the Craft are found in Pennsylvania and New England, the first so-called anti-Masonic sentiment is recorded. The "Pennsylvania Gazette," No. 444, June 9 to 16, 1737 — published by our Bro. Benjamin Franklin — relates how Dr. Evan Jones, a prominent apothecary of Philadelphia, duped an apprentice, Daniel Reese, who had expressed a desire to become a Freemason. Seeing an opportunity for ribald amusement, Dr. Jones and several associates put the young man through some absurd ceremonies, telling him he was an Entered Apprentice, and directed him to return June 13, 1737, for another degree. Further horse-play, coupled with indecencies and indignities, were then indulged in. These were followed by a final ceremony in which his Satanic Majesty appeared, but who, to the disappointment of the conspirators, did not serve to frighten the candidate; whereupon Dr. Jones, the impersonator of the devil, threw a pan of flaming spirits upon the apprentice, with such frightful effect that he died three days later.

The publication of the story in local papers, and the blame attached to the regular Masons, innocent of any wrong doing and equally strong in their censure and condemnation of the act, brought the fraternity into bad repute in certain quarters, and enemies of the local Craft did not hesitate to seize upon the occasion to further their own ends. The various accounts were reprinted in the colonial papers, and thus the occurrence achieved a place in the annals of American Masonry as the first anti-Masonic expression in the colonies.

Aside from the excitement and feeling engendered in Philadelphia by the regrettable occurrence, it had no serious effect. Sporadic expressions are found in later years which only serve to indicate that Freemasonry was well established. One Christian Sauer, an erratic printer of Germantown, took a fling, in 1740, at the free school system inaugurated by Benjamin Franklin, and vented his spleen upon it by saying: "The people who are promoters of the free schools are Grand Masters and Wardens among the Freemasons, their very pillars."

An early reference to the Craft from an anti-Masonic standpoint appeared in the New York Mercury of Dec. 31, 1753, in which considerable space is given to the assumption of office by George Harrison as Provincial Grand Master. The occasion was made noteworthy by the donation of fifteen pounds toward the purchase of clothing for poor children in the charity school; an additional sum was raised for indigent prisoners. This prompted the editor to ask:

Query. Whether the performance of public and private acts of beneficence, such as feeding the hungry and clothing the naked, be most correspondent to the Genius of Christianity, or the Institution of the Prince of Darkness?

There were no direct attacks the Craft in Massachusetts until 1751. The Pennsylvania affair and the anti-Masonic activities of European enemies were impartially recorded in the papers of the colony. On Jan. 7, 1751, some doggerel verse and a picture were printed in the "Boston Evening Post" of a very disgusting nature. The brethren of Boston were much disturbed thereby, and passed resolutions in local lodges and also in Grand Lodge against the publication.

With this brief introduction, the subject of Anti-Masonry in the American Colonies can be dismissed for present purposes. It was not until the last decade of the eighteenth century that we encounter what may be termed anti-Masonry in the strict sense of the term, and which really had a marked effect upon the Craft. The roots of the Morgan Affair of 1826 are found herein, and the student going into the subject thoroughly will find much hitherto unconsidered material to examine.

ANTI-MASONRY IN EUROPE

The anti-Masonic spirit, which developed in the period of 1797-1825, had its foundation in the literature avowedly written to oppose secret societies in Europe, which were accused of being anti-Christian, anti-social and dangerous to both state and religion. Freemasonry was unavoidably included among the leading societies of the period, for the fraternity had made a rapid growth throughout Continental Europe from the day it was first introduced in England.

Space forbids a presentation of the background attached to the story of Anti-Masonry in Europe; let it suffice to say for present purposes that the French Revolution, 1789-1799, was watched in this country with both interest and anxiety. Many of our people were in open sympathy with the French, and Genet, the French minister accredited to our government, was enthusiastically received by these. The French popular customs were imitated, French revolutionary songs were sung, the American and French colors were displayed together. The French Jacobin clubs were imitated by the formation of democratic associations styled "Democrat Clubs," and the phrase, "the rights of man," was heard at assemblies of all kinds.

The course of Washington in proclaiming strict neutrality, even though not endorsed by many of our citizens, saved this nation from dangerous consequences. The details can be learned from any reliable history; we are only concerned with the influences which bear upon the development of anti-Masonry. These are found in the principles of Jacobinism. Briefly, the Jacobins of France were originally members of a political club formed in 1789 which was not extremely radical, but which underwent rapid changes until the term "Jacobinism" became synonymous with the promulgation of extreme revolutionary opinions. The conservative members were excluded by internal processes until the club degenerated into a loosely defined but very dangerous organization, which brought about the reign of terror in France under Marat and Robespierre at the very time (April, 1793) that Washington issued his neutrality proclamation. The horror of the period stirred the civilized world to its depths. Genet, in America, misinterpreted the popular opinion, and in his enthusiasm threatened to appeal to the mass of the American people if our leaders did not permit activities which were threatening to involve us in war with Great Britain. Popular sentiment thereupon began to weaken; Genet was recalled in disgrace by his government, which would have beheaded him had he returned. He was permitted to remain in the United states, and later married the daughter of Governor De Witt Clinton (a Mason) of New York, dying at an advanced age.

The aristocracy and the Roman Catholic clergy suffered the greatest losses during the French Revolution. It was but natural, therefore, that they should attempt to fasten the responsibility upon some one. The Jacobins, representing the masses, were pointed out as the instigators of the misfortunes which had befallen the upper classes. One of the representative literary productions of the period was the *Memoires poui servir a l'histoire du Jacobinisme,* by Abbe Augustin Barruel, published in French in London in 1797. A second edition followed in 1798; English translations were available immediately. The work was also printed in German; numerous abridged editions appeared each year from 1798 to 1802. It was printed in Spanish as late as 1827.

An American edition, four volumes, was published in Hartford, Conn., "printed by Hudson & Goodwin for Cornelius Davis, New York," in 1799.

ROBINSON'S PROOFS OF CONSPIRACY

A work akin to Barruel's, written independently of it, was Proofs of a Conspiracy against all the Religions and Governments of Europe, carried on in the Secret Meetings of Free Masons, Illuminati and Reading Societies, by John Robinson, A. M., Edinburgh. It was announced in January, 1797, two editions appeared some months later, a third of 1798 was reprinted in Philadelphia the same year. New York and Dublin editions of 1798 are also known. Like Barruel's work, this, too, was reprinted in other languages,

French and German editions predominating, with one printed in Holland, no date given. Barruel acknowledged the priority of Robinson in Vol. III, p. xiv, London edition of 1798; Robinson refers to Barruel in his second edition, page 519.

Barruel and Robinson asserted that secret societies were responsible for the distressing situation in Europe, and did not hesitate to place the odium upon the Freemasons and the Illuminati. Thinking people accepted these statements seriously. Says Hayden:

The public mind in the United states was not only agitated with the aggressions of France, which threatened a bloody war between our country and our former ally, but also that the cause of the frenzied state of the public mind in France, and other parts of Europe, was ascribed to Masonry under the name of Illuminism. France, in her folly, had attempted to banish every vestige of revealed religion from her domain, and had caused it to be inscribed over the gates of her churchyards that death was an eternal sleep. False tongues were not wanting to say that Masonry designed to overturn all human governments. (1)

The Illuminati referred to were members of a secret society founded in Bavaria in 1776 by Adam Weishaupt, professor of canon law at the University of Ingolstadt. Its object was:

By the mutual assistance of its members to attain the highest possible degree of morality and virtue, and to lay the foundation for the reform of the world by the association of good men to oppose the progress of moral evil.

Weishaupt, who became a Mason between Nov. 26, 1776, and Feb. 8, 1777, adapted Masonic rites and customs to his society; but the activities of Jesuit enemies caused its suppression by royal edicts in 1784 and 1785. Weishaupt fled to Gotha and found protection under Duke Henry II, devoting his energies to the writing of philosophical treatises.

INFLUENCE IN AMERICA OF THE LITERATURE OF THE PERIOD

The periodicals of England and America graphically related the startling French occurrences to their readers, and it was upon such, supplemented by personal correspondence, that non-participants based their opinions. This was particularly true in America. The causes of a colossal disturbance are always sought for; whether the reasons given be right or not, supporters of various claims can always be found. The Barruel and Robinson books contributed to the available information — and misinformation. Freemasonry was charged by some to be at the root of the difficulties, (2) and it can be perceived readily that a growing acceptance of the charge would make the publication of anti-Masonic literature profitable. It must be remembered that the general public was not so familiar with Freemasonry as it is today, the secrecy always associated with the fraternity was not only restricted to its essential words, signs and grips which are the sum total of actual Craft esotericism, but was also construed to cover membership, places of meeting and the like. Therefore, literature purporting to expose the "secrets" of Freemasonry found a ready sale among the curious and the gullible, and also, in the times under discussion, among earnest, serious and conscientious persons imbued by a legitimate desire to be informed on a subject of more than ordinary moment. The gamut of interest ranged between the two extremes.

The elusive reference to be found in the ephemeral literature of the period need not be stressed herein; the interest lies in the more enduring publications. Among those are the numerous editions of Jachin and Boaz, an alleged expose which first appeared in England in 1762, and was reprinted by the thousand from that year down to the present day. No doubt many copies circulated in the Colonies. The first American edition which has been traced is one of 1796, printed in New York city. It was followed by others in New York, Pennsylvania and New England in the years 1797, 1798, 1802, 1803, 1811, 1812, 1814, 1815, 1817 and 1825; probably there are editions which have escaped the Masonic bibliographer. One in Spanish was printed in Philadelphia in 1822.

The exposes mentioned thrived in the soil fertilized by the Barruel and Robison volumes. An abridgement of Barruel and Robison appeared in 1802, at Charlestown, Massachusetts, entitled Proofs of the Real Existence and Dangerous Tendency of Illuminism, by Seth Payson, A. M. One of the Barruel volumes was reprinted in 1812 at Lancaster, Pennsylvania, in a volume entitled *Antichristian and Antisocial Conspiracy* which also contained within its covers a reprint of Jachin and Boaz.

BEGINNING OF CLERICAL OPPOSITION

The situation in France was viewed with continued alarm by our representative citizens when John Adams became the second President of the United states. Saying, among other things, that the United States was "at present placed in a hazardous position," he issued a proclamation on March 23, 1798, proclaiming May 9, 1798, as a public fast day. Rev. Jedediah Morse, Charlestown, Massachusetts, preached a sermon on that occasion which opened the way to long and inflamed discussions of the Illuminati, and indirectly upon Freemasonry. The Rev. Morse made no allusions to the Craft in his sermon, but his silence on the subject was noted as peculiar and significant when his listeners later read the Robison book which he had recommended to them in his sermon. Other comment followed in the pulpit and the newspapers. College presidents and political orators discoursed volubly upon the new menace to civilization. The cry had been raised, and the pack was in full chase.

A dissenting voice dared to question the assertions and the insinuations that had been made. "Censor," writing in the Massachusetts Mercury of July 27, 1798, asked for proofs. The Rev. Morse, looked upon as the proper person to answer the query inasmuch as he had been the first to arouse public interest through his sermon, was not loath to take up the fight. Yet he expressed surprise that he should be called upon to substantiate statements (Robinson's) which contained such excellent internal evidence of their truth.

He was astonished, among other things, by the sensitiveness and irritation which the Masons had displayed; he had hoped that the manner in which he handled his sermon would preclude censure from that direction. The controversy waxed warm; Morse spoke again in a formal address on Thanksgiving Day, 1798. He was supported in his position by clergymen in other pulpits; the numerous Thanksgiving sermons revived interest in the subject and it swept through the countryside. The public did not differentiate With meticulous care between secret societies in general and the Craft in particular; the resentment and denial of Freemasons that they had nothing to do with the Illuminati fell on inconsiderate ears. They had been linked together, and that was all that was necessary to make them avowed allies. The Grand Lodge of Massachusetts, in protest, drew up an address to President Adams on June 11, 1798; it stated its position relative to civil authority and declared that Freemasons promoted the public welfare. The reply of President Adams is worthy of record herein:

Many of my best friends have been Masons, and two of them my professional patrons; the learned Gridley and my intimate friend, your immortal Warren, whose life and death were examples of patriotism and philanthropy, were Grand Masters; yet, so it has happened, that I had never the felicity to be initiated. Such examples as these, and a greater still in my venerable predecessor (Washington) would have been sufficient to induce me to hold the Institution and Fraternity in esteem and honor, as favorable to the support of civil authority, if I had not known their love of the fine arts, their delight in hospitality, and devotion to humanity.

The Rev. Thaddeus Harris, Grand Chaplain of the Grand Lodge, delivered some stirring addresses, in one of which he blamed the clergy for the prevailing Illuminati excitement. He spoke of them as those "who ply the shuttle-cock of faith, with the dexterity of expert gamesters, and have the art of making the multitude fly with its feathers." The Grand Lodge of Vermont also went on record (Oct. 23, 1798) in dignified defense of the Fraternity.

Adams appointed a second fast day, set for April 25, 1799. Morse seized upon the occasion to voice his opinions upon the subject into which he had precipitated himself by his previous Fast Day sermon. In his address—the third and last—he called attention to some alleged Masonic correspondence, showing a connection between the Grand Orient of France and bodies in America, situated at Portsmouth, Va., and presumably at New York, as well as in the French possessions in the West Indies. Apparently, Masons were Masons the world over, and that fact was sufficient to brand the American Craft as a danger to the government and all social institutions. (3)

JEFFERSON'S COMMENT ON BARRUEL

Yet in spite of the clerical opposition from Morse-and it must be remembered that there were brethren of the cloth in. New England who did not agree with him, and even opposed his utterances — the diatribes fell flat. The political dangers pointed out did not hold ground; Thomas Jefferson, although not a Mason, went so far as to comment on the absurdity of the Barruel books held forth by Morse as authorities and proofs. Others rallied to the assistance of those who declared Morse's position untenable, and it was not long before the hue and cry subsided. The Masonic angle was definitely cleared away by a letter showing that the lodge at Portsmouth, Va., was a reputable organization, and its members honest and industrious citizens of the community. Morse wisely refrained from further discussion, and politically, at least, the attacks failed. The danger to the Craft was over from that direction until after the disappearance of Morgan, when numerous attempts were made to revive the alleged connection of Freemasonry with the Illuminati of the previous century. Noteworthy in this connection were two seceding Masons, Moses Thacher and Henry Dana Ward, both of whom were ministers.

A review of the Masonic press for the few years preceding the Morgan Affair of 1826 shows that there was marked opposition to the Craft from Protestant clerical sources; but before citing a few of the many instances that can be found, mention should be made of one cause contributed by Freemasons themselves. The Masonic writings and orations at the period (1800-1825) reveal a boastfulness that reacted seriously after 1826, and which gave the enemies of the Craft weighty matter in support of anti-Masonic utterances. This spirit of braggadocio and arrogance continued to within the very year of the Morgan abduction. Early in 1826, the "Christian Telescope," a religious paper edited by Rev. David Pickering and published by Barzillai Cranston, both Masons, in commenting on an Alabama anti-Masonic situation, said:

We are truly thankful to find this spirit of intolerance confined to the bigots of Tuscaloosa, who will find it hard to kick against a Colossus, which, if it had the inclination, could crush them or any other denomination of sectarians, almost without an effort, that is in America, where civil and religious liberty have established a dominion.

This was quoted from a Wilmington, North Carolina paper, said to have been edited at the time by Rev. Jacob Frieze, also Grand Chaplain of the Grand Lodge of Rhode Island.

The most glaring examples of such Masonic boasting prior to the Morgan Affair can be found in the expressions of William F. Brainard. His lecture before Union Lodge, New London, Connecticut, on Saint John's Day, June 24, 1825, was probably quoted more by anti-Masons than any other similar addresses. The following is a good example of his indiscreet and uncalled for remarks:

What is Masonry now? It is powerful. It comprises men of rank, wealth, office and talent, in power and out of power, and that in almost every place where power is of importance, and it comprises, among the other classes of the community, to the lowest, in largest numbers, effective men, united together and capable of being directed by the efforts of others so as to have the force of concert through the civilized world. They are distributed, too, with the means of knowing one another, and the means of keeping secret, and the means of co-operating; in the desk, in the legislative hall, on the bench, in every gathering of men of business, in every party of pleasure, in every enterprise of government, in every domestick circle, in peace and in war, among enemies and friends, in one place as well as in another.

So powerful indeed is it at this time, that it fears nothing from violence either public or private, for it has every means to learn it in season to counteract, defeat and punish it.

REJECTIONS AND EXPULSIONS WERE FACTORS

Another cause for enmity against the Craft was the unusually large number of rejections and expulsions. The latter were published in the Grand Lodge proceedings of the time; and considering that reading matter was not so profuse as it is now, and that the Craft was a far greater mystery than it is today, it can be readily assumed that the publicity thus accruing to the expelled brethren was pronounced. The resentment welling therefrom in the hearts of rejected petitioners was far more intensive than the feelings engendered in modern times through similar actions. Such individuals would be inclined to join anti-Masonic demonstrations, rather than hold aloof.

A corollary to such rejections and expulsions is the apologetic attitude of Masonic speakers, who, taking cognizance of the prevailing but yet lightly provocative anti-Masonic sentiment, still offered a defense of the Craft. Rev. John L. Blake, A. M., speaking before Friendship Lodge at Gloucester, Rhode Island, in 1825, said:

In view of the remarks made, it may well be concluded, that Masonry is, in no sense, opposed to Christianity, notwithstanding that many nominal Masons are a disgrace to the name they bear.... The person who is a dishonor to the Christian church is no honor to the Masonic Fraternity. It may be asked then, if the good Mason is not almost the good Christian!

Henry Gassett, a virulent anti-Mason of his day, points out in the introduction to his Catalogue of Anti-Masonic Books (Boston, 1852) that anti-Masonry existed "in Hamilton College, New York, in 1819, and in the Presbyterian Church of the United states, in 1820" (page 84). Rev. John G. Stearns, a writer of anti-Masonic literature after the Morgan Affair had taken place, had been made a Mason in Champion Lodge, No. 146 (New York). Stearns, in citing his reasons for issuing his Inquiry Into the Nature and Tendency of Speculative Freemasonry, had the following to say:

In the fall of 1819 I was received as a student in the Literary and Theological Seminary of Hamilton, N.Y. In my examination I was inquired of whether I was a Mason. I answered in the affirmative. I was then requested to dispense with Masonry while a member of that school. I replied that I ad already made up my mind never to have anything more to do with Masonry.

EXAMPLES OF RELIGIOUS OPPOSITION

Just as at the present time we have some narrow and bigoted religious Protestant sects, so in the days under discussion preachers were not lacking who believed that Christianity's cause was promoted by assailing alleged evils. The seeds furnished by Morse and his kind — sincere and honest as they were in their beliefs — were transmitted to the outlying settlements of Pennsylvania and Western New York by itinerant preachers and circuit riders and found fertile soil. It was they who kept alive the distrust of all secret societies long after the political menace of such organization from abroad had faded into nothingness. The Roman Catholic opposition, such as has developed in a more pronounced manner since the Morgan Affair, was either negligible or non-existent. The Roman Catholics were not large in numbers or influence; where attention was directed toward them — as in Ohio by Henry Ward Beecher in the thirties and forties-they were classed with the enemies of Americanism. The charge was made — one that no person would advance today — that Freemasons were allied with Roman Catholics "to crush the liberty of the Republic." An able illustration of the blindness of popular prejudices and passion! (4)

The "American Masonic Register and Ladies' and Gentlemen's Magazine" (New York), for January, 1821, carries this notice:

The Western (Pennsylvania) Register says — "We are informed that at the last meeting of the Presbyterian Synod of Pittsburg, some of the clergy introduced a resolution to exclude Freemasons from the rights and benefits of the Church, except in case where they might confess their errors, and abjure their Masonic principles."

In its issue of March, 1821, a full account is given. It is of value to the student as showing the sentiment against the Craft, for it is evident that it was prepared after careful deliberation. After a preliminary statement of some length, the committee drafting the report recommended that the following resolutions be adopted:

1. Resolved, That Masonic lodges, especially as composed and conducted in various parts of our country, have had, and are calculated to have, a pernicious influence on morals and religion, and that attendance on them is unsuitable to the profession of the holy religion of our Lord Jesus Christ, Therefore—

2. Resolved, That it is the duty of all ministers of the gospel, elders, parents, and professional Christians, to use their influence to prevent those under their care from entering these associations, and induce those who may have entered, to discontinue their attendance.

3. The synod, deeply impressed with concern for the general interest of society, civil and religious; particularly with concern for some amiable men, who now stand connected with the aforesaid society, recommend them to take with earnestness the course of safety for themselves; and in the present crisis of the conflict of the kingdom of God with the kingdom of darkness, to show themselves on the Lord's side, and to perform zealously, the duties which their attitude in relation to the church of Christ, and to those societies, particularly recommend; so as not only to promote the cause of godliness generally, but also the eternal welfare of their brethren, with whom they may be connected, and upon whom they may exert a salutary influence.

It should be pointed out, however, that the report was not adopted by the Synod; still it has its value herein as showing the marked and organized opposition to the Masonic Fraternity at that time in religious circles. The lodges of Pittsburg took cognizance of it, as shown by a lengthy article quoted by the American Masonic Register, from the Pittsburgh Gazette.

The Tuscaloosa incident of 1826 previously mentioned herein relates to the action of Methodists at Tuscaloosa, Alabama, publicly resolving "that the cause of God, in their opinion, could not prosper while connected with Freemasonry." According to Charles McCarthy, the General Methodist Conference of Pennsylvania had taken action in 1823 forbidding its ministers from becoming Masons.

The Masonic Mirror and Mechanic's Intelligencer (Boston, May 6, 1926) calls attention to the proscription of Masons by Methodists, yet points out that many of the New England Methodists are "zealous and good Masons." The issue for Oct. 14, 1826—it should be remembered that the Morgan Affair was not mentioned in its columns until a month later—states:

We learn from the Kentucky Gazette, that an inquisitorial bench has been erected by the South District Association of Baptists at Salt-River, Mercier county, in that state, for the trial of their minister for the "horrible crime" of being a FREEMASON !

As one reads the Craft literature of the period, he is further impressed with the fact that both subtle and marked opposition to the Fraternity existed. To illustrate: An address delivered June 24, 1818, to the brethren of Washington Lodge, No. 17, Hamilton, Ohio, by Bro. William Burke (printed in full in the "American Masonic Register" for July 21, 1821), has three columns addressed "To the Members of Religiouis Denominations" in which a defense of the Craft against one of the clerical aspersions is made. Other instances could be cited, increasing in number a approach the Morgan Affair, and, of course, appearing still more frequently after that occurrence. The point to be made is that anti-Masonic sentiment was strong for many years before the disappearance of Morgan. It was that sentiment which made it possible for shrewd political opportunists to further their own ends with such a simple and preposterous occurred as the Morgan Affair.

NEW YORK GRAND LODGE POLITICS

Another factor to be considered in the anti-Masonic sentiment of the pre-Morgan period is the political situation in the Grand Lodge of New York. The two factions struggling for supremacy at the time brought undue notoriety to the Craft in the state through their efforts to increase factional strength by increasing the number of lodges, and the membership of both old and new lodges among the supporting elements. To quote R. W. Bro. Charles W. Moore, Grand Secretary of Massachusetts, an active and outspoken Mason during the excitement of 1826-40, and who was editor from 1842 to 1873 of the "Freemasons Monthly Magazine":

Canvassers, either by appointment, or as volunteers, were active in all the western counties, and persons were urged to come into the Institution, who had no more right or claim to be there than they had to be in any other good place, or to associate with honorable men. They were brought in, forced in without the payment of any money, but on notes and due bills and when the time came for a settlement and a readjustment of the pending difficulties, and a reunion of the bodies, thousands of dollars rolled into the Grand Lodge in due bills, that had never been paid, and which there had never been any intention to pay. (5)

This laxness was one of the causes of the 1826 difficulties and also had an influence in the unprecedented withdrawal of members from the Fraternity when the storm burst in full force. Bro. Moore supports the statement that the clergy took a dominating part in the excitement. On this subject, he said:

The anti-Masonic excitement soon worked itself into all neighboring towns, broke up many of our lodges, spread dissension in the churches, and demoralized too many of our clergy, too many (God knows, too many) of whom, trampling their obligations under their feet, joined our enemies, and, in many instances, did us more harm than all the opposition arrayed against us.

NOTES

(1) From a MS. in the archives of the Grand Lodge of Maryland.

(2) The assertion that Freemasonry was involved in the tragic development of the French

Revolution is shown to be unfounded when it is recalled that the Jacobins suppressed all Masonic lodges. It was not until Napoleon assumed authority that the Freemasons were permitted to assemble again.

(3) Mention should be made at this point of the Act of Parliament, July 12 1799, "for the more effectual Suppression of Societies established for Seditious and Treasonable Purposes " etc. The situation in France, and in Ireland, was specifically mentioned therein. Enemies of Freemasonry mentioned the Act, even though Masonic lodges were exempted from its provisions. (See Gould, *History of Freemasonry*, Vol. II, pages 486-88; also Acts of Parliament Referring to Freemasonry London, 1847 and 1817.)

(4) "In view of the well-known attitude of the Catholic Church in regard to Masonry, it is really remarkable how little Catholics in the United states seemed to mix in this fierce strife. Ann Royall, the most widely known woman of her day and country (1769-1854)-traveler, author, editor and lecturer-said they 'minded their business' and she respected them accordingly. But Presbyterians, Baptists and Methodists fell greatly under her displeasure because of their hostility toward Masonry." *Life and Times of Ann Royall*, by Sarah Harvey Porter, M. A., 1909, page 107

(5) Proceedings of the Grand Lodge of Massachusetts, 1871, page 417.

BIBLIOGRAPHY

For the history of anti-Masonry in the Colonies, the reader is referred to Julius F. Sachse's *Benjamin Franklin as a Freemason* (Philadelphia, 1906); Sachse and Barratt's Freemasonry in Pennsylvania (Philadelphia, 1908), and Melvin M. Johnson's *Beginnings of Freemasonry in America* (New York, 1924).

Extensive histories of the United States cover the French Revolution insofar as it affected our country during Washington's and Adams' administrations. The "Gentleman's Magazine," London, June, 1794, contains an attack on Freemasonry, to which answer is made in "The Masonic Essayist," part two of *Masonic Miscellanies in Poetry and Prose*, by Stephen Jones, London, 1811. Freemasonry and the French Revolution is a subject by itself. *New England and the Bavarian Illuminati*, by Vernon Stauffer, Ph. D., New York, 1918, treats of the Illuminati phases; this is No. 1, Vol. LXXXII of "Studies in History, Economics and Public Law," published by the Columbia University Press. The Robison and Barruel books have been listed by their full titles in this article.

The addresses of Rev. Thaddeus Harris, Grand Chaplain of the Grand Lodge of Massachusetts are available in *Discourses on Public Occasions* (Charlestown, 1801, and Philadelphia, 1819; also London, 1847-50)..

Among the Masonic periodicals of the period which have been consulted are "The Masonic Miscellany and Ladies' Literary Magazine," Lexington, Kentucky, 1822; "The American Masonic Register and Ladies' and Gentlemen's Magazine," New York, 1821 et seq., "The Masonic Casket," Enfield, New Hampshire, 1823-25; the "American Masonick Record and Albany Saturday Magazine," Albany, New York, 1827-32; the "Masonic Mirror and Mechanics' Intelligencer," Boston, 1824-27, and others.

The Proceedings of various American Grand Lodges have contributed material of value, notably those of Massachusetts, 1871. Material was also gleaned from numerous pamphlets and brochures published between 1827 and 1840; these will be cited in the articles in later bibliographical notes.

THE SPIRITUAL SIGNIFICANCE OF FREEMASONRY
by Silas H. Shepherd

The most essential thing for every Freemason to learn is just what Freemasonry is, and how it functions. The ritual contains all that is necessary to a very clear and comprehensive knowledge, but in many cases those who participate in the forms and ceremonies of the ritual fail to carefully analyze the things they hear and see, and even those who assume to teach sometimes fail to fully understand the words and sentences they have memorized.

We are told that Freemasonry is a "regular system of morality veiled in allegory, which will unfold its beauties to the candid and industrious inquirer." It has also been defined as "the subjugation of the human that is in man by the Divine; the conquest of the appetites and passions by moral sense and reason; a continual effort, struggle and warfare of the spiritual against the material and sensual." Another very beautiful definition is that it is "a union of unions, an association of men, bound together in their struggles to attain all that is noble, who desire only what is true and beautiful, and who love and practice virtue for its own sake." Many are the definitions that might be quoted to show the high importance and spiritual significance of Freemasonry. Methods of expression differ, but every student of Freemasonry is agreed that its forms and ceremonies are but a means and method of bringing man to a better comprehension of the real purpose of life, and to develop the qualities of his soul.

We often read in Masonic books and periodicals that Freemasonry is not a religion. "A religion" implies one of several or many religions, and in this respect Freemasonry is most emphatically not a religion. If we accept the definition of religion as the outward act or form by which men indicate recognition of a God to whom obedience and honor is due, we cannot well deny that Freemasonry is positively and basically religious.

It will be readily conceded that any person who desires to become a member of the Fraternity has little conception of its serious purposes. He is, however, given a fairly comprehensive idea in the formal petition he signs, and again in the questions to which he must give unequivocal answers. These questions are of first importance. If the answers are sincere and strictly lived up to, the candidate will not only become a member of the organized Fraternity, but will also be a Freemason in its most comprehensive sense. He will learn to subdue his passions — fear, hate, greed, selfishness, prejudice, intolerance, anger, envy — and improve himself in the science of character building. These questions, which every Freemason answers in the affirmative, are so important that we believe every candidate ought to not only memorize them but frequently question himself as to whether he is strictly complying with them:

Do you seriously declare, upon your honor, that, unbiased by friends and uninfluenced by mercenary motives, you freely and voluntarily offer yourself a candidate for the mysteries of Freemasonry ?

Do you seriously declare, upon your honor, that you are prompted to solicit the privileges of Masonry by a favorable opinion conceived of the institution, a DESIRE FOR KNOWLEDGE and a SINCERE WISH OF BEING SERVICEABLE TO YOUR FELLOW CREATURES?

Do you seriously declare, upon your honor that you will cheerfully conform to all the ancient established usages and customs of the Fraternity?

These are serious obligations voluntarily assumed, and no deviation can be made without moral retrogradation. We repudiated mercenary motives and declared our desire for knowledge. What kind of knowledge ought we to expect? Surely not that which pertains to our financial, material or physical welfare. The knowledge we can rightly expect and surely find is a knowledge of our moral and spiritual nature, and is to be used in being serviceable to our fellow creatures.

If we have gone thus far and failed to comprehend the deep spiritual significance of Freemasonry, the address of the Junior Deacon to the candidate ought to put everyone in the proper attitude for the impressive ceremonies. This also is of such importance that frequent rehearsal of it is greatly to be desired.

"Mr. _____, the institution of which you are about to become a member is one by no means of a light and trifling nature, but of high importance and deep solemnity. Masonry consists of a course of ancient hieroglyphical and moral instructions, taught according to ancient usage, by types, emblems and allegorical figures. Even the ceremony of your gaining admission within these walls is emblematical of an event which all must sooner or later experience.... You are doubtless aware that whatever a man may possess here on earth, whether it be titles, honors or even his own reputation, will not gain him admission into the Celestial Lodge above; but, previous to his gaining admission there, he must become poor and penniless . . . dependent on the sovereign will of our supreme Great Master."

Can there be any further doubt that Freemasonry is appealing to the soul of man? The esoteric ceremonies of reception ought fully to satisfy us, but for the purposes of this essay we are only using the monitorial portions. The prayer at the reception of a candidate might alone give us the very keynote of Freemasonry.

"Vouchsafe Thine Aid, Almighty Father of the Universe, to this, our present convention. Grant that this candidate for Masonry may dedicate and devote his life to Thy service, and become a true and faithful brother among us. Endue him with a competency of Thy Divine wisdom, that by the secrets of our art he may be better enabled to display the beauties of Brotherly Love, Relief and Truth, to the honor and glory of Thy Holy Name. Amen."

The Masonic brethren who established this great nation on the principles of Liberty and Equality placed their trust in God. They placed a motto, "In God we trust" on the coins of the country. Freemasonry stresses not alone a belief in God, but a trust in God. No lodge is ever opened or closed without invoking Divine assistance.

The Holy Bible, that great light in Masonry, is the most conspicuous article of furniture of a lodge. It is the first thing which is intrusted to the care of the Master at his installation and he is told that it "will guide you to all truth; it will direct your paths to the temple of happiness, and point out to you the whole duty of man."

"The Holy Bible is to rule and guide our faith." The English lodges call it the Volume of the Sacred Law, and Mackey, in his use of it as a Landmark, calls it the Book of the Law, because he says it is not absolutely required that everywhere the Old and New Testaments shall be used. "Masonry does not attempt to interfere with the peculiar religious faith of its disciples, except so far as relates to the belief in God and what necessarily results from that belief. The Book of the Law is to the speculative Mason his spiritual Trestle-board; without this he cannot labor; whatever he believes to be the revealed will of the Grand Architect constitutes for him this spiritual Trestle-board, and must ever be before him in his hours of speculative labor, to be the rule and guide of his conduct."

These quotations from the monitorial parts of the verbal ritual are only helpful hints at the possibilities that lie hidden in the symbol and allegories. These are only hidden from those who fail to follow up their expressed "desire for knowledge" with the necessary industry and zeal to acquire it. Nothing in Freemasonry is ever hidden from those who are worthy and properly prepared. Our hearts and souls are the soil in which the seed must germinate. Not only must we be industrious as physical and intellectual beings but we must be industrious spiritually if we are to "divest our minds and consciences of the vices and superfluities of life, thereby fitting us as living stones for that spiritual building, that house not made with hands; eternal in the heavens."

We find three principal systems of symbolism in Freemasonry. First, the building of a spiritual Temple by the use of symbolic tools. Just as surely as the operative workman can erect a temporal structure by the tools and implements of architecture, so we can erect a beautiful Temple of Character if we will use the tools of our speculative science as we are taught. No great cathedral was quickly built, neither can we expect to erect within ourselves a perfect character without long continued and persistent effort. By the constant practice of the one tenet of Brotherly Love, we may make daily progress.

Brotherly Love is not only a beautiful ideal, but an actual fact in nature. It is our failure to live in conformity to it that causes most of the discord and confusion in the world. We profess to believe in it. We profess to regard the whole human species as one family. Unless we practice it we are failing to practice Freemasonry. By their fruit shall ye know them.

The search for the lost word. The quest of the Holy Grail. The endless search for truth and light which never ceases from the cradle to the grave. The symbolism of the lost word has taught countless Masons the usefulness of searching for the Truth. God's Infinite Truth is not comprehensible to our finite minds. As we prepare ourselves by soul development we receive as much as we deserve.

Lastly, Freemasonry teaches by an allegory of unsurpassed beauty the great lesson that our bodies are but the temporary shelter of our soul, and after passing through the experiences necessary the dust returns to its Mother Earth and the soul returns unto God who gave it.

"It was the single object of all the ancient rites and mysteries practiced in the very bosom of pagan darkness, shining as a solitary beacon in all the surrounding gloom and cheering the philosopher in his weary pilgrimage of life to teach the immortality of the soul. This is still the great design of the Third Degree of Masonry."

It is in the light of this teaching that the Master Mason, raised to the eminence of that "Sublime Degree" can look back on the Charges he received as all Entered Apprentice. Then, the precepts of the Moral Law were symbolically expounded by authority; now, in the further light afforded him, he sees the reason for what; before he took on trust, and is thereby fitted to guide others in his turn.

ROSICRUCIANISM IN FREEMASONRY
by H.V.B. Voorhis

There seems to be a decided interest in Rosicrucianism springing up among Masonic students. The mystery of the Rosy Cross, as it is more generally known, is apparently becoming more mysterious. (The terms Rosicrucian and Brother of the Rosy Cross are in reality synonymous, but the first term often intimates a reference to the "Order" itself, while the second connotes a relationship to the Rose Croix, now the Eighteenth Degree of the Scottish Rite of Masonry.) This revival of interest manifests itself every few years with added zest and is caused, usually, by a new investigator appearing upon the horizon with new (or at least more) facts; combined also with the a certain activity within the modern Rosicrucian societies.

Lately I have perused several important writings containing opinions on the existing complex and conflicting data related to this obscure subject. These show, to my own satisfaction at least, that the history of Rosicrucianism and Freemasonry has a common spiritual descent, a common mystery and at one time, during the early years of the two movements, had a common motive.

The mere mention of the word "Rosicrucian" in occult circles immediately produces an atmosphere of awe. Individuals who are the most sound logicians in every other branch of research, almost without exception begin to float on air, and, for the most part, enjoy it, as soon as this subject is broached. As Arthur Edward Waite has said:

"Perhaps there has never been a realm of inquiry which has been colonized to such an extent by fools and knaves of speculation. If there has been one other, it is that which adjoins with no intervening boundary - I mean Emblematic Freemasonry.

The reason for this condition is not difficult to see. It is a condition of mind, resulting from the perusal of the many works on the subject by the great students who have written so deeply and voluminously on not only the subject of Rosicrucianism itself, but also on the outstanding men and, in a few instances, the women involved in the manifold workings of "The Order of the Rosy Cross."

It would almost seem that every person of note as an occult scholar from the year 1500 to 1800 (and possibly further) has been in some manner connected with the "Order." Independent schools of or allied to Rosicrucianism have developed an individual literature for each school - thus complicating the development of a system rather than clarifying it.

Says Waite:

"The great spiritual symbolism which has come down to us through several houses of tradition, is not, I think, communicated in a plenary sense by any one school; it is rather the harmony of all.

A sentence once written in the thirteenth century by that unsurpassed thinker, Roger Bacon, can be applied very pertinently to Rosicrucianism. He said:

The subjects in question are weighty and unusual, they stand in need of the grace and favor accorded to human frailty . . . for I am speaking of the sophistical authorities of the irrational multitude, men who are authorities in an equivocal sense, even as the eye carved in stone or painted on canvas has the name but not the quality of an eye.

The eminent English Mystic, Waite already quoted, says further:

The touchstone is always life, and for this reason antiquity per se is not a test of value. There would be no Hidden Mystery of the Rosy Cross if it had not suffered successive transmutations, adjusting a change of venture to a new heart of motive. I think, indeed, that it has died many times and has been as often reborn, even a little "nearer to the heart's desire."

Anderson, whose *Book of Constitutions* was first published in 1723, gives a source for Masonic origins of which many subsequent writers have availed themselves down to the present day. The representations made by these good brethren of earlier days do not bear critical analysis in some respects, in spite of the fact that we do not question their motives nor the sincerity of their beliefs. One statement concerning the origin of Freemasonry has to do with its beginnings in the Garden of Eden, for Anderson says:

Adam, our first Parent, created after the Image of God, the Great Architect of the Universe, must have had the Liberal Sciences, particularly Geometry, written on his Heart; for even since the Fall, we find the Principles of it in the Hearts of his Offspring, and which, in process of time, have drawn forth into a convenient Method of Propositions, by observing the Laws of Proportion taken from Mechanism: So that as the Mechanical Arts gave occasion to the Learned to reduce the Elements of Geometry into Method, this noble Science thus reduc'd, is the Foundation of all those Arts (particularly of Masonry and Architecture), and the rule by which they are conducted and perform'd, etc., etc., etc.

In the dedication of The Constitution, J. T. Desaguliers, Deputy Grand Master, takes pains to say that he needed not to tell his Grace of Montagu, to whom it was addressed,

. . . what Pains our learned AUTHOR has taken in compiling and digesting this Book from the old RECORDS, and how accurately he has compar'd and made everything agreeable to History and Chronology, so as to render these NEW CONSTITUTIONS a just and exact Account of MASONRY from the Beginning of the World to Your Grace's MASTERSHIP.

The views of Anderson, and those of later writers who followed him blindly, or elaborated upon the beauteous concepts of their times, are no longer accepted. In fact we are hard put to prove our existence prior to the Norman Conquest, and it is not until we reach the year 1390 A. D. that we first find documentary evidence - the *Regius Poem*, also known as the *Halliwell MS.*, now preserved in the British Museum. A few of these early Old Charges are the only definite evidence we have.

Rosicrucianism, however, has numerous documents relating to its activities, and especially during the two centuries prior to the year 1717, when speculative Freemasonry established this date as the foundation stone of a new dispensation. If we accepted the evidence offered by Spencer Lewis, the Rosicrucian Order can be traced back to King Thothmes III, B.C. 1500. However, let us put aside this speculation as to very ancient origins and content ourselves with the later history.

It cannot be refuted that, in the century prior to the formation of the premier Grand Lodge of England, many eminent men were practicing Rosicrucianism, not only in England but also in Germany, France, Holland and possibly other countries.

The word "Rosicrucian" first appears in print in 1614, and shortly thereafter the so-called Order first took form as a permanent organization through a man known as Christian Rosenkreutz whose date of birth appears to have been about 1378, although his Fama and Confessio did not attract attention until two hundred and fifty years later upon its original publication. (1)

There is no exact period of commencement of the Rosicrucians as an Order, as there is in Freemasonry. Every well informed Mason recognizes the date 1717. There can be no misunderstanding that at that time the first Grand Lodge of Masons appeared. The best we can say about Rosicrucianism is that Rosy Cross literature appeared in German and Latin between 1614 and 1616 - affirming that a secret and mysterious Order had existed in Germany for some two centuries. These writings marked the entrance of Rosicrucianism into the daylight of contemporaneous criticism and attack.

To acquaint those interested with this branch of learning, Thomas De Quincy, in 1824, wrote a work entitled Historico-Critical Inquiry into the Origin of the Rosicrucians and the Freemasons. While this served as an excellent introduction to the subject, it was, to quote Waite, a mere transcript from an exploded German savant, whose facts are tortured in the interest of a somewhat arbitrary hypothesis.

The first serious treatment of the subject in English, from an historical standpoint, was Hargrave Jennings' *The Rosicrucians, Their Rites and Mysteries*, 1870. It had gone into many editions and is still a so-called textbook on Roscrucianism. The two-volume edition of 1887 is considered the most desirable.

This treatment has been superseded by the *Real History of the Rosicrucians*, 1887, by Arthur Edward Waite and by another work written many years afterward on this subject from the pen of the same author (really his magnum opus), *The Brotherhood of the Rosy Cross*, 1924. This book is a most exhaustive treatise, especially in the treatment of the material whereof this so-called "Order" is built. There is at least one excellent work in another language by Fr. Wittemans, D.L., covering the history of the Rosicrucians - but, so far, it is not available in English.

In America a writer, whose work on this subject in connection with Freemasonry has been taken seriously, is Brother Ossian Lang, Grand Historian, of the Grand Lodge of New York State. A small pamphlet reprinted from the proceedings of the Grand Lodge of New York, 1918, written by Brother Lang, gives data purporting proof of a Rosicrucian derivation of Freemasonry.

In the recent work of Manly P. Hall, the subject of Rosicrucianism is taken up by the author in the chapter headed "The Fraternity of the Rosy Cross," by formulation of four postulates. The material has been carefully selected from a very wide range of works and excellently arranged.

Rosicrucianism first appeared in Germany (in the City of Cassel) in the latter part of the sixteenth century and came into public light, as already mentioned, in 1614. After arousing a great deal of interest in that country for about ten years, the mysteries of the Rosy Cross died down, and, because of the departure of several of the Rosicrucian adepts to India (2), the struggle for "thought freedom" was shifted to the Netherlands, where it had been going on slowly for a quarter of a century. Persons of the highest classes of society met in palatial structures under the Rosicrucian banner at both Amsterdam and The Hagu in 1622. Some of these persons ran afoul of the law of the land and were haled into court on various charges.

About this time, according to Wittemans, Frederic Henry, Stadtholder, who leaned toward the occult, and who no doubt saw a "writing on the wall," shifted his protection from Rosicrucianism to Freemasonry (3).

In France there was no Rosicrucian activity until about 1623, when, after a first public announcement, the Rosicrucians became embroiled in arguments with the Jesuit Fathers. Descartes and Abbe de Villars were about the only two flaming spots of French Rosicrucianism of this period and, as they have not the slightest connection with Freemasonry, we turn our attention to England.

Concerning Rosicrucianism in England, Wittemans remarks that:

The efforts of the Rosicrucians to erect a new spiritual temple of humanity, which failed in Germany, the Netherlands and France, were destined to be crowned with success in England. In the latter country the free development of human thought was not hampered by orthodoxy and, there, resulted in a spiritual movement that afterward found expression in Freemasonry, the universal temple of wisdom and fraternity.

Some time between 1614 and 1620, according to Waite, Robert Fludd, an English philosopher, physician, chemist, mechanic, anatomist, mathematician and astrologer, having been influenced by Maier became a "convert" to Rosicrucian thought. He at once began writing on the subject and there appeared in 1616 his Apologia, a defense of Rosicrucianism. This was followed by a dozen or more other works on Rosicrucianism over a period of some twenty years. There are some (Dr. W. Wynn Westcott, for instance) who believe that Fludd was the first English Magus of the Brotherhood. At any rate, Fludd, together with Lord Verulam, better known as Francis Bacon, formed an English Rosicrucian Society in which Bacon, though secretly, played the principal role.

Bacon was 57 years old when Elias Ashmole, the famous English astrologer, was born and of whom we have positive proof of his being "made a Freemason" at Warrington in 1646. Bacon, however, died in 1626 at the age of 65 years, without, so far as we have any positive evidence, ever having been "made a Freemason."

Bacon is believed by many to have been the real author of the works attributed to Shakespeare and to have superintended the English translation of the Bible. He was the author of many works of a philosophical nature. His only connection with our story, however, is in relation to certain theories advanced by various writers that Freemasonry was either partially or totally shaped by him. To such Waite says:

"The attempt to explain Freemasonry - Emblematical, Speculative and Figurative - as a new birth in time of the Order of the Rosy Cross has passed into desuetude, and yet there is evident - for it manifests now and again sporadically - a certain unsatisfied feeling, as if the last word still remained to be said. So also is there a feeling that in some way, occult and unproven, a shaping influence was exercised by Francis Bacon, Lord Verulam, on the first beginnings of the Masonic Order. I do not suppose the last word has been said on this subject either, but it is clear to my mind that it must be one of negation This thesis was started by Nicolai, in an appendix on the origin of Freemasonry attached to an Essay on the Knights Templar. The foundation is Bacon's unfinished romance *The New Atlantis*, written late in life and published posthumously."

This view is not taken by either Fr. Wittemans or the Rev. F. de P. Castells of England. Bro. Castells, who is engaged at present on works concerning the origin of the Masonic degrees, supports, with modifications and amplifications, the views of Mrs. Henry Pott as advanced in her Francis Bacon and His Secret Society. Fr. Wittemans says:

"He [Bacon] ranks first among those who made Freemasonry heir to the Rosicrucian philosophy, at the time when the Masonic body underwent a reformation in the XVIIth century."

Manly P. Hall contributes this information:

"Johann Valentin Andreae is generally reputed to be the author of the Confessio. It is a much-mooted question, however, whether Andreae did not permit his name to be used as a pseudonym by Sir Francis Bacon. Apropos of this subject are two extremely significant references occurring in the introduction to that remarkable potpourri The Anatomy of Melancholy. This volume first appeared in 1621 from the pen of Demoeritus Junior, who was afterward identified as Robert Burton who, in turn, was a suspected intimate of Sir Francis Bacon. One reference archly suggests that at the time of publishing The Anatomy of Melancholy in 1621 the founder of the Fraternity of R. C. was still alive. This statement - concealed from general recognition by its textual involvement - has escaped the notice of most students of Rosicrucianism. In the same work there also appears a short footnote of stupendous import. It contains merely the words: "Joh. Valent. Andreas, Lord Verulam." This single line definitely relates Johann Valentin Andreae to Sir Francis Bacon, who was Lord Verulam, and by its punctuation intimates that they are one and the same individual."

As Robert Macoy, the well-known Masonic writer, believed that Andreae was the true founder of Rosicrucianism, so, following the reasoning of Mr. Hall, indications appear that Bacon was responsible for even more than is generally suspected in the launching of our project. Further references along similar lines are found in Godfrey Higgins' Anacalypsis, and in the writings of the late Frank C. Higgins.

No matter which view one considers correct, it is most certainly a fact that Bacon lived at a time in which the minds of the forefathers of organized Masonry had their setting - a time in which it appears that English Rosicrucianism waned and Freemasonry assumed its outward role and continued on - and, according to Bro. Castells, soon worked out its role.

To go into this matter further would entail a complete review of Waite's, Castells', Mrs. Pott's and Fr. Wittemans' works, to say nothing of those quoted in this article. One must refer the reader to the writings of these individuals if interested in obtaining the latest views thereon. Wittemans' book, as indicated, is, unfortunately, not yet available in English.

The Rosicrucian connection with Freemasonry was considered in Quatuor Coronati Lodge, No. 2076, of London, in a paper written by Dr. Wynn Westcott in 1894 (4).

Edward Conder, Jr., Waite, Van der Gon, Alting, Raemaekers, Mrs. Pott and Castells all agree that Bacon and Rosicrucianism certainly had something to do with Freemasonry just prior to its "revival" of 1717. But so many opinions have been expressed on various phases of the subject that to cite any here would be burdensome reading.

Fr. Wittemans estimates that over twenty thousand books and articles have been written on Bacon's alleged authorship of Shakespeare's plays. It would be natural to suppose that there would also be an extensive literature on the Baconian theory of Masonic origin. Just the reverse however, is true. Although there is a distinct school of the Bacon-Masonic origin theorists, it is supported by but few writers, and their contentions have received but meagre support.

Many writers endeavor to prove that the Rosicrucians used many symbols traceable to ancient Masonry. This department of our subject is even more confusing, especially to minds not trained in symbology, but it cannot be denied by anyone familiar with the "teachings" of both " fraternities " that many similarities do exist. Basing their judgment on things symbolic, De Quincy and Buhle believed that Freemasonry was Rosicrucianism modified by those who introduced it from Germany into England.

Because of changes in ritual after the formation of the premier Grand Lodge, before which time Freemasonry and Rosicrucianism were supposedly closely allied, and the organization of the present or modern Rosicrucian societies, which appear to lack descent from the original "Order," those differences have broadened.

The recent work of Bro. Castells (5) has again brought these questions to the fore among Masonic students. Coupled with the fact that the Rose Croix Degree has been drawn into the discussion, we have the outpourings of the English and American societies working under the banner and the name of Rosicrucianism, so that the present period promises some interesting research into these absorbing topics.

Freemasonry is defined as "a beautiful system of morality, veiled in allegory and illustrated with symbols . . . Truth is its center. It is founded on the purest principles of Morality, Brotherly Love and Charity," which Rosicrucians "have aimed to produce, in the crucible of spiritual alchemy, the perfect Man, who loves God above all, on whose heart the Christ has awakened and who has become a pillar of love and wisdom among his fellowmen," says Wittemans.

Where one "system" leaves off and the other begins cannot be precisely defined - like a mixture of water and glycerin, no one can tell by vision which is more in quantity. Rosicrucianism and Freemasonry, it seems, were once entwined. Since that time each has perceptibly changed in both spirit and matter. If they were definitely separated once, much more must be known to determine their points of separation. Even now their forms are not easily separated. The teaching of each "system" is not a clear and defined thing. Students of either school fail to present a positive agreement in aims or objects - and even less, the students of both.

The writer has not set down the above in a disparaging sense, but just the reverse. He has read many works on both subjects and feels that studies of this nature are far more important than the grinding out of meaningless "joining Masons. " In fact, he feels that works such as Fr. Wittemans, are permanently valuable and hopes that this publication will be translated into the English language in the near future, so that it may take its proper place beside the work of Waite, Castells, Hall and others cited above. It is by far the most thorough and comprehensive work of its kind that has come to my attention and makes an excellent companion volume to Waite's *The Brotherhood of the Rosy Cross*. Its value, particularly to Masonic students, as well as to students of the Rosy Cross, lies in the great clarification it makes of the subject it covers.

NOTES

(1) *The Fama Fraternitatis*, which is believed to have been written in the year 1610, but which apparently did not appear in print until 1614, although an earlier edition is suspected by some authorities. Manly P. Hall, *An Encyclopedic Outline of Masonic, Hermetic, Qabbalistic, Rosicrucian and Symbolic Philosophy*, 1928.

(2) See the notes on the Latin pamphlet by Henrieus Neuhusius, 1618, in Waite's *Occult Sciences*, 1891, p. 210.

(3) Certain data in the work cited concern an ancient Masonic lodge in Amsterdam of great antiquity, have a bearing on this subject, and may bring out some interesting light on Freemasonry in the Netherlands.

(4) "The Rosicrucians, Their History and Aims, with reference to the alleged connection between Rosicrucians and Freemasonry," A. Q. C. vol. vii, p. 37.

(5) The works by the Rev. F. de P Castells referred to are his *Antiquity on the Holy Royal Arch*, 1927; the *Origin of the Masonic Degrees*, 1928; and *The Historical Analysis of the Holy Royal Arch Ritual*, 1929.

THE NEW ATLANTIS AND FREEMASONRY
by A. J. B. Milborne

Among the many theories of the origin of Freemasonry, is that which advances the hypothesis that: it was the outgrowth of the plan of Francis Bacon to accomplish a regeneration of mankind by the introduction of a state of civilization similar to that depicted in his The New Atlantis published in 1627.

This theory was advanced by Christopher Frederick Nicolai, a learned German savant, in a work published in 1782 3 entitled, *An Essay on the Accusations Made Against the Order of Knights Templar and Their Mystery; With an Appendix on the Origin of the Fraternity of Freemasons*. It has never obtained any acceptance at the hands of Masonic students and critics, for the recognized existence, after subjection to every literary and critical test, of The Old Charges for two hundred years prior to the publication of Francis Bacon's romance is sufficient evidence to refute it.

Nevertheless, bearing in mind the fact that many distinguished men of letters and science founded the Royal Society a few years after the death of Bacon with the object of disseminating scientific and philosophical truths on the basis of his suggestions and the further fact that members of the Royal Society were prominent in the revival of the Craft which culminated in the formation of the Grand Lodge in 1717, the consideration of *The New Atlantis* from a Masonic standpoint is not to be neglected.

THE ALLEGORY

The New Atlantis is a narrative which deals with the fabled island of Bensalem in the Pacific Ocean and the culture and customs of its inhabitants. Its main feature, Solomon's House, is the embodiment of Bacon's lifelong dream of finding some method or system by means of which scientific knowledge could be accumulated and used for the amelioration of mankind, for he writes "among all the benefits that could be conferred upon mankind, I find none so great as the discovery of new arts, endowments and commodities."

The setting of the tale was suggested by Plato's myth of Atlantis, contained in the Timaeus, and the writer has also drawn on the Critias which contains a description of the origin and splendid civilization of this fabled country. The New Atlantis gives us very little information about the constitution of the country, its laws or the structure of its society, for Bacon laid down his pen when he had dealt with the many wonders of Solomon's House, not because the chief interest of the story was then exhausted, but, as Rawley writes in the Preface to the Latin version, "because he had many other matters which deserved to take precedence of them" (i.e., *The New Atlantis* and another unfinished work — *the Dialogue Concerning an Holy War*). The form of government may be taken, however, as being an ideal commonwealth though differing from the communistic conception of Plato. Here, then, we find an analogy with the Masonic Lodge which symbolically represents the universe and an ideal government based on the brotherhood of man, with the recognition of distinctions "necessary to preserve subordination."

THE DISTRESSED VOYAGERS

The romance opens with a description of the plight in which the company of a ship finds itself. The ship had sailed some months previously from Peru for China and Japan, and after five months of favorable winds had been driven off its course by adverse ones. The food supplies had become exhausted and sickness had broken out, when the voyagers come in sight of land. They approach it and enter a harbor, and are about to make a landing, when the inhabitants make signs to them not to do so. In the reception of the voyagers we find a ready compliance with the duty of rendering to our fellows those kind offices which justice or mercy require, for while the Bensalemites forbid them to land, they tell them to write down their wants and they would "haue that, which belongeth to mercy."

The narrative goes on to relate the written answer given to the Bensalemites and that, three hours later "a Person (as it seemed) of place" approached them in a boat and desired that some of the visitors meet him upon the water, which was done, and the subsequent interrogation "Are yee Christians ?" and the humble confidence which it inspired bears a close analogy to our reception of a candidate. After giving an oath "by the Meritts of the Saviour" that they were not pirates and had not shed blood, lawfully or unlawfully "within fourtie daies past" they were informed that on the following day they would be brought to the "Strangers' House" which was an institution akin to our modern Quarantine Station, though not so irksome for the only limitation placed upon the newcomers was to remain within doors for three days, after which they might visit the city, though they were not to go more than a mile and a half from the city walls without special leave.

On the expiration of the three days the voyagers were visited by a Christian Priest, who informed them that he was the Governor of the Strangers' House, and offered them his services "both as Strangers, and chiefly as Christians." He told them that the state had given them permission to remain for six weeks, but that an extension might be obtained, if desired, and that if they wished to trade they would be fairly dealt with.

THE ARK CONTAINING THE SCRIPTURES

The next day the Governor of the Strangers' House came to them and explains that by reason of their isolated position, the laws of secrecy by which they were bound, and their rare admission of strangers, the Bensalemites were well acquainted with the greater part of the habitable world, but were themselves unknown, and goes on to say, "Therefore because he that knoweth least, is fittest to ask Questions, it is more Reason, for the Entertainment of the time, that yee aske mee Questions, then I aske you." They then inquire who was the Apostle of the Nation, and how it was converted to the Christian faith, and the Governor, in reply, relates the reception of a "small Arke, or Chest of Cedar" containing "all the Canonicall Bookes of the Old and New Testament" and a letter written by Saint Bartholomew in which he states that he had been warned by an Angel to commit the Ark to the sea. This is probably based on the tradition recorded by Eusebius, "the Father of Church History," that Saint Bartholomew had left a copy of St. Matthew's Gospel with the Indians.

The following day the Governor answers further questions as to how the Bensalemites were so well informed of the world's affairs while the world remained in ignorance of their existence, but he reserves some particulars "which it is not lawfull for mee to reueale." He tells of the great amount of navigation of the earlier days, the intercourse of the various nations and then of the destruction of the Great Atlantis. Proceeding, the Governor relates the difficulties of "the poore Remnant of Humane Seed" which survived the inundation, the history of King "Salamona" and the code of laws which he put into force. "Doubting Nouelties" King "Salamona" prescribed certain "Interdicts and Prohibitions" one of which concerns the admission of strangers. Those who laid the foundation of the Masonic Order have also given us certain regulations regarding the admission of strangers, and, "doubting novelties" have prohibited any change in our established usages and customs which has received universal recognition as a primary landmark of the order.

SOLOMON S HOUSE

The raison d'etre of the romance—the order or society of Solomon's House—is next outlined. The Governor refers to it as "The Noblest Foundation . . . that euer was upon the Earth" dedicated to the study of the works and creatures of God—("the hidden mysteries of nature and science")— and named by King Solomon "finding himselfe to Symbolize" after the King of the Hebrews. The method of obtaining information of the outer world by the sending of Missions of three of the fellows or brethren recalls to our mind the despatch of the trusty fellowcrafts by King Solomon, divided into three lodges, upon a certain mournful quest. The brethren of Solomon's House are termed "Merchants of Light," which has its parallel in the expression "Sons of Light" as applied to Freemasons.

The voyagers now lived quite happily, and the narrator tells us that they went abroad seeing what was to be seen in the city and places adjacent "within our Tedder." "Tedder" is the middle English form of the word "tether" and we find a similitude in the Masonic cable-tow.

The Feast of the Family, granted to any man who lived to see thirty descendants alive together "and all above 3 yeares old" is then minutely described. In the description of the room in which the feast is celebrated we find a symbolic emblem similar to one with which Master Masons are familiar in the decoration of the "state" of canopy over the chair in which the Tirsan as "the father of the family" is termed is seated. The concluding part of the ceremony attending the feast is the presentation to any of the Tirsan's sons of "eminent Merritt and Vertue" of a jewel "made in the figure of an Eare of Wheat" a symbol which we preserve in the Fellowcraft degree to remind us of those temporal blessings of life, support and nourishment which we receive from the Giver of all Good.

The rest of the book is taken up with a description of the customs of the country and concludes with a full recital of the many wonders of Solomon's House, a remarkable forecast of the inventive genius of man.

It is generally conceded that one of Bacon's principal achievements was the impetus given through this work to thought in England, which resulted in the formation of the Royal Society not many years after his death Glanville said that Solomon's House was a prophetic scheme of the organization that has done so much for the advancement of science, and Boyle, one of its earliest and most famous members, spoke of an "in visible college" in his letters, which probably referred to the beginnings of the Society before its formal constitution in 1660. The attempt has been made to definitely connect Bacon with the Speculative reorganization of Freemasonry; the fact that some of the founders of the Royal Society were Masons is certainly a curious coincidence, but whether we can ever go further than this is doubtful.

THE FORTY-SEVENTH PROBLEM OF EUCLID
by C.C. Hunt

The Master Mason will readily recognize this proposition as one of the emblems of the Third Degree. He will also recall the monitorial explanation of it there given, and possibly feel that it is an explanation which does not explain. He may not question the legendary history of it as given to him, but he does not understand why it should have been selected as a Masonic emblem, nor how it teaches Masons to be lovers of the arts and sciences. In fact there are many Masons who are not mathematicians and do not even know what the proposition is, and on this point the monitor is silent.

It is the object of this paper to briefly consider the history of the proposition and offer a few suggestions as to its Masonic significance. In doing this we may reach the conclusion that some of the monitorial statements are not historically true, or at least that they have not been proven. We will find, however, that the value of its symbolism does not depend on the truth of the historical statements given in the monitors, but is inherent in the proposition itself.

This will be hard for many Masons to understand. Through association of ideas, we are accustomed to think that the traditions which cluster around a central truth, are essential parts of that truth, and when critical investigation attacks the truth of the tradition, we feel it is an attack upon the truth itself. It is this trait of human nature which is the underlying cause of all religious persecution, and we are by no means free from it as Masons, though it is contrary to the fundamental principles of Masonry.

It is our duty to search for the truth, no matter how much it may conflict with our preconceived notions or with traditions. If we but search aright, we will find that these traditions are but the outer garments with which time has clothed the truth, and that they are not its essential essence.

In our associations with each other we meet a kindred soul whom we learn to love and honor. We are told that he is the descendant of a great and honored name in history, and we say that the spirit of his forefathers has fallen upon him. Then some critic appears and shows that there is no proof of his illustrious ancestry, or perhaps entirely disproves it. What of it? Is he not the same friend we knew before? Has his soul lost any of its greatness? May not the spirit of a great soul have descended upon him, though his physical blood does not literally flow in his veins? We are told that the spirit of the prophet Elijah descended upon Elisha and centuries later appeared in John the Baptist. Yet there was no blood relationship between them. So it is with the proposition we are now studying. Its tradition and its history are both interesting, but its truth and the richness of its symbolism are not affected thereby.

In Euclid's *Elements of Geometry* there are thirteen books, and the subject we are considering is the forty seventh proposition of the first book. It is not a problem but a theorem, and is so called by Euclid. A problem in geometry is something to be done, as a figure to be drawn, while a theorem is something to be proved. This proposition is to prove, as Euclid states it, that "In any right-angled triangle, the square which is described on the side subtending (opposite) the right angle is equal to the square described on the sides which contain the right angle." The sides containing the right angle are called respectively the base and perpendicular, while the side opposite the right angle is called the hypothenuse.

Our monitors state that "This was the invention of our ancient friend and brother the great Pythagoras." This statement has been denied by many students of the subject. It has been claimed that this proposition was known to the Egyptians long before the time of Pythagoras, and that he learned it from them and carried it into Europe and Asia. We have no proof either for or against this claim. Pythagoras himself wrote nothing, and we know of his teachings only through the writings of his disciples. Vitruvius, a celebrated Roman architect of the time of Augustus Caesar, attributes the discovery of this proposition to Pythagoras. Plutarch quotes Apollydorus, a Greek painter of the 5th century B.C., as authority for the statement that Pythagoras sacrificed an ox on the discovery of this demonstration. Proclus credits Pythagoras with the first demonstration, but asserts that his proof was different from that given in Euclid. In fact so many writers, both ancient and modern, have attributed this proposition to Pythagoras that it is commonly called by his name, "The Theorem of Pythagoras."

On the other hand, the properties of the triangle whose sides are respectively, 3, 4, and 5, were certainly known to the Egyptians and were made the basis of all their measurement standards. We find evidence of this in their important buildings, many of them erected before the time of Pythagoras. We also find that this triangle was to them the symbol of universal nature. The base 4, represented Osiris, the male principle; the perpendicular 3; Isis, the female principle; and Horus, their son, the product of the two principles, was represented by the hypothenuse 5.

May we not find an explanation of this apparent discrepancy in the statement of Plutarch that Pythagoras discovered the demonstration of the general proposition, but that the particular case in which the lengths of the sides are 3, 4, and 5, was earlier known to the Egyptians? Plutarch also thinks that the case in which the base and perpendicular are equal (as in the sides of a square) was likewise known to the Egyptians. This is called the classical form in Masonry and is the form usually found on the Master's carpet. Both these forms are rich in symbolism, and if known to the Egyptians, as they probably were, would naturally lead to the belief that the general demonstration was also known. Nevertheless it may be true, as claimed by so many writers, that to Pythagoras we owe the demonstration of the general proposition, which proved the theorem true for all possible cases. It was the delight of this philosopher to discover a universal principle underlying a concrete fact, and he must have attached a deeper meaning to the general truth than the Egyptians did to the special cases known to them. With him the science of numbers was the essence of all truth, and having discovered a proof for the general proposition, he set himself the task of finding right triangles whose sides can be expressed in numbers. Heron of Alexander and Proclus are authority for the statement that Pythagoras discovered the following method: Take any odd number for the shortest side; subtract one from the square of that number and divide the result by two; this will give the medium side; add one to the medium side and the result will be the hypothenuse or longest side. This is true as far as it goes, but it does not give all the right triangles which can be expressed in numbers.

The numerical symbolism of Pythagoras is an interesting study in itself and is closely allied to much of our Masonic symbolism, but that is outside the province of the present paper. It is simply mentioned here, because, while it is probably not true that he was raised to the sublime degree of a Master Mason as stated in our monitors, yet there is so much resemblance between his teachings and that of Masonry, that we can understand how the error might have occurred.

The monitor also states that Pythagoras celebrated his triumph in the discovery of this proposition by the sacrifice of a hecatome (one hundred oxen). We can see how this may have been an outgrowth of the statement attributed to Apollodorus above. Ovid denies it and Hegel laughs at it, saying, "It was a feast of spiritual cognition, at the expense of the oxen." The strongest argument against it, however, is the fact that Pythagoras taught the doctrine of the transmigration of souls and forbade animal slaughter. However, when we consider that among many of the ancients the sacrifice of a number of oxen was their method of expressing their gratitude for a great triumph, we can understand how the tradition arose, and accept the fact of the joy without caring for the truth of the sacrifice.

Why should the discovery of this demonstration have been considered a great triumph? Because it is of the utmost importance to the science of geometry. Dionysius Lardner, in his edition of Euclid, quoted by Mackey, says, "Whether we consider the 47th problem with reference to the peculiar and beautiful relation established in it; or to its innumerable uses in every department of mathematical science, or to its fertility in the consequences derivable from it, it must certainly be esteemed the most celebrated and important in the whole of the elements, if not in the whole range of mathematical science. It is by the influence of this proposition and that which establishes the similitude of equiangular triangles (in the sixth book) that geometry has been brought under the dominion of algebra; and it is upon the same principle that the whole science of trigonometry is founded." The Encyclopedia Britannica calls it "One of the most important in the whole of geometry, and one which has been celebrated since the earliest times ;" and adds, "On this theorem almost all geometrical measurement depends, which cannot be directly obtained."

What is its significance in Masonry? Our monitors tell us that it teaches Masons to be lovers of the arts and sciences. Since it is so important a proposition in the science of mathematics, we can understand why it should be adopted as a symbol of scientific investigation, and to such an investigation all Masons are pledged in their search for truth, the great object of Masonic study. But has it not a deeper meaning? Dr. Lardner says it is the basis of the application of algebra to geometry. Algebra is the application of symbols to mathematics, and Masonry is the application of symbolism in character building. *The Britannica* says that mathematical measurements which cannot be directly obtained depend on this proposition. Yes, and as applied to Masonry, the highest truths of morality cannot be directly obtained. They must come to us indirectly through the medium, principally, of symbolism.

There is no apparent relation between the numbers 3, 4, and 5 and 5, 12, and 13, for instance; but when we raise these numbers from the first to the second power (that is, square them), we obtain 9, 16, and 25 in the first case, and 25, 144, and 169, in the second. In this form we notice in each case that the sum of the first two squares is equal to the third, and that the numbers in which we could at first see no relation are the sides of right angled triangles. So it is in life. Measured on the level of our lower natures, there is no relation between our own desires and our brother's needs. We are connected, it is true, as the sides of a triangle are connected, but there is no reason why we should not use him for the accomplishment of our own selfish purposes, irrespective of his welfare. It is only when we square our lives by the square of virtue, and our selfish desires are raised to spiritual purposes, that we perceive that our own welfare is intimately connected with that of our brother. His misfortunes are our misfortunes, and we can no more injure him and not be ourselves harmed thereby, than we can strike off our right hand and be none the worse by reason thereof.

We are traveling upon the level of time to our eternal destiny. We cannot stand still, but must constantly go forward. Shall we also go upward ? All the time there is a spiritual force striving to lift us to higher levels. We may refuse to avail ourselves of it and remain in the depths of our lower nature; or we can accept it and allow its divine influence to shine in our lives. The base represents our earthly nature on the level of time; the perpendicular is the divine spirit striving to manifest itself through us. When these forces are squared to each other, their union becomes a constant onward and upward movement to the throne of God Himself. Pythagoras himself recognized this symbolism when he said that early in life he came to the place where two ways parted. One was easy and pleasant traveling; the other was rugged and tended upward. It necessitated hard climbing. Which was the way that led to life ? All who travel there and find these two paths, know that he should choose the upward path, but the other seems so much more pleasant, and many are inclined to walk therein. They will try it a little while, and then return to the better way. But there is no turning back on the level of time. The farther they go on the lower level, the wider apart become the two ways, and the harder to cross from one to the other.

How often we have heard Masons say that there is no moral lesson to be derived from the 47th proposition of Euclid, and that it is not to be described as the symbol of any moral truth. Have they forgotten that there is not an observance or symbol of Masonry which has not a deep significance? Significance for what? Certainly as Masons it would have no especial significance for us unless it aided us in attaining the great purpose of our Order, "the uprearing of that spiritual temple, that house not made with hands, eternal in the heavens." It may well be that the significance is not recognized by us, but that by no means proves its nonexistence. It may be buried in the rubbish of preconceived opinions, and it only needs diligent digging to bring it to light.

We have here suggested but a few of the many applications of this symbol in the hope that it will stimulate others to more diligent research.

MASONRY AND WORLD PEACE
by Joseph Fort Newton

Had anyone written a story of modern civilization last spring, it would have read like a romance. What a picture it would have painted of the triumphs of art and industry, of disease yielding to the skill of science, of the intellectual linking of nations, of the rapid march of ideas, of the annihilation of time and distance by the ingenuities of invention. The bright cities of the earth, with their palaces of art and prayer, lay bathed in sunlight. Aircraft explored the sky, and wireless messages flew every whither, telling of the glory of man.

And then — a high-school boy in remote Bosnia fired a pistol, and a pall of ancient barbaric night fell over the earth, darkening the heavens. Merciful God! The tragedy of it — beyond comparison the greatest war in all the long annals of time in the new century! In an instant, all trace of civilization seemed to vanish, and nation was leaping at the throat of nation, filling the world with measureless misery and woe. Commerce languishes, art is paralyzed, religion is mocked, and civilization seems tumbling to a fall. Four days of the cost of this conflict would dig the Panama Canal and pay for it. One month of it would equip every hospital on earth to fight the great White Plague. Of the loss of life, the most precious of all wealth, who can think without a sob, remembering the cold law of biology by which, if the fittest fall, only the weak remain to father the men of times to be.

What man may ever hope to find words wherewith to tell the shame, the crime, the pity of it all. Prating of Evolution, we were swept along on the crest of an easy optimism, not realizing that we were carrying with us the lower forms of life, "moods of tiger and of ape, red with tooth and claw." Well may we refresh our memories by reading that passage in the "Republic" of Plato, in which a Pagan philosopher laid down the rules of civilized warfare, as follows — non-combatants to be spared, no houses to be burned, no farms to be devastated, the dead to be honorably buried, no trophies of war to be placed in the temples of the gods. What a rebuke to Christian civilization in a day when shrines of art and learning and piety are ruthlessly destroyed, and men act like fiends incarnate! Indeed, a page from the story of this war reads like an excerpt from the chronicles of Hell, as witness these words from a warlord to his men: "Cause the greatest possible amount of suffering, leave the non-combatants nothing but their eyes to weep with. The law of Christian charity has no bearing on the relation of one nation to another."

— II —

With the immediate causes of this world-shaking war we have not here to do, except to say that no matter what generalization we make about it, there will be found as many facts on one side as on the other. History will debate them for ages to come. Any investigation into the question of who fired the first gun promptly goes back into the question of who made the gun, and why ? Who diverted the beautiful, constructive energy of human-ity into such wanton waste and unreason ? After reading the many-colored books put forth by the nations, each in its own defense, we may admit that all are right in their reasonings, if we accept their basic fallacy that a nation is a thing apart from humanity to be hedged about with walls of iron.

They are nearer the truth who look for the roots of this tragedy in the ideas taught by unphilosophic philosophers within the last decade or two. Ideas rule the race. They run like rumors, they hide in the crooked lines of a printed page, but in the end they force us into the arena to fight for them. Materialism in philosophy led, naturally and inevitably, to a worship of brute Force, bringing scientific efficiency to the service of all the horrible gods of sport and speed and splendor. Offering incense to the diabolical trinity of Mammon, Mars, and the Minotaur, we have become so vain of our material advance and scientific technique that we have forgotten that hu-man well being lies in the pursuit of justice and brotherly love. With Neitzsche preaching atheism in the alluring style of a poet, while Treitschke and Bernhardi expounded a rationale, if not a religion, of war, 'tis no won-der that we have been brought to where we are, to a cataclysm unbeliev-able, except that it exists.

This is not to cry down modern inventiveness and its astonishing achievements. Far from it. Not one of us but feels the thrill of this amazing effort, albeit often futile and misdirected, to realize life. There can be no question that this is a wonderful age, romantic in its advance. Equally, there can be no question that things still more wonderful are to follow. But what is it all worth — this "will to power," this conquest of Nature — if it lead to a wide weltering chaos of world-war ? To be sure, we travel more rapidly and get news more quickly, but, God of dreams, what news of savagery and slaughter! No; our ideals are wrong, and with all the suffering and ruin already wrought, maybe it will get into our brains, and at last into our hearts, that our real progress does in fact depend on the genuine love of God and our fellow man. Only in tragedy, it seems, will man learn the highest truth.

Still, if we would find the real causes of this dreadful war we must go far back and deep down into the nature of man. Human history is saturated with blood and blistered with tears. It has been estimated that in the annals of mankind, there have been only thirteen years when there was no war on earth. "Men are only boys grown tall, Hearts don't change much, after all. Nations are these lads writ large, That's what makes the battle charge."

So reads the record of the ages, and we cannot hope to reverse that order of things in a day. Envy, ignorance, jealousy, greed, hate, revenge, vanity, racial rancor, love of strife, these make war against peace. Nevertheless, we must refuse to accept war as the permanent condition of human society. Slavery was once well nigh as universal as war, if not as old, but it has been banished from the earth. We cannot look forward very far, but, despite the horror of today — perhaps, indeed, because of it — there is reason to hope for a time when war, and the menace of war, shall be removed from the terrors of human life.

— III —

What the issue of this gigantic conflict will be, no mortal can tell. One hundred years ago Europe was swept bare by wars of might against right, yet out of that long-drawn tragedy came a great advance of civilization. So it may be, must be, will be now. Make no mistake; the right will triumph, and as one nation after another is released from the burden of militarism, the arts of peace will prevail, the democratic spirit will be extended, and civilization will, in the end, be promoted. History, always the sure cure for pessimism, holds out this hope even to those, if such there be, who see above its tangled and turbulent scene no vaster, wiser Power correcting the blunders of man, and "from seeming evil still educing good in infinite progression."

Amidst all doubts, one thing is certain: kings may pass, dynasties may vanish, but the peoples of Europe will remain substantially as they are within their historic boundaries. But these battered and impoverished peoples will be preserved for no other purpose than new wars and new disasters if they do not fit themselves with a nobler, truer way of thinking. More important than all else is the question, not as to the map of Europe, but as to what the map of the human mind is going to be after the war. How well men have learned war, reducing it to a fine art of destruction, is shown by those great guns that speak with throats of thunder, and those "airy navies grappling in the central blue," as Tennyson predicted. Now they must learn peace, which means that they must begin with the young, and keep always at it, until mankind masters the sweeter, truer, and diviner language of fraternity.

In point of fact, we have been trying to do an impossible thing — trying to found a humane order upon a basis of brute force. It cannot be done. Long ago Greece built its structure of art and life upon a basis of slavery, and it fell. Just so, our civilization will fail and fall if it is built upon a foundation of Force. After all, it may be that this war was an inevitable result of a transition from the rule of Force to the rule of Numbers, and, ultimately, the rule of Reason and Love. One is tempted to hope that, since it had to come, it will not stop until all despotisms are swept away, and with them all upholding of the privilege of the few against the rights of the many; until men everywhere rise up and say they will not go to war unless they have a vote on war. John, Hans and mystic Ivan will strike or soon or late, and then will come the end of Kings and Kaisers — and if this war hastens that day it worth all it cost!

As the grand divisions of geological history have their beginnings in stupendous revolutions, so, too the great new epochs in the human world. Such a time is even now with us. Manifestly, we stand at the end of an era, and the men who come after us will wonder that, seeing, we saw not, and mistook the red dawn of a new day for a house on fire. As Napoleon would say, we are condemned to something great. Whatever betide, the old order has collapsed. The times are infinitely plastic. There is no reason for letting go of faith in God or human kind. Instead, those who have eyes will see in this tempest a storm that shall clear the air of pestilential vapors and hasten the advent of a nobler world-order, through the corrected sense of the nations — the final flaring up of a blaze from falling brands, to be covered forever with penitential ashes and quenched with bitter tears.

IV

Meantime, what has Masonry to say, what can it do, in this hour of world-crisis when the race is struggling through blood and fire toward something new, shaking off shams, and coming face to face with the eternal necessities? Forming one great society over the whole globe, bringing men together without regard to race or religion, it is incredible that this Ancient Order should be inactive, much less indifferent, in a day of supremedemand.

From the first Masonry has been international, knowing no Slavic race, no Teutonic race, but only the Human race, in proof of which hear these words from its Book of Constitutions — words that stand out like stars in the night of world-feud: "In order to preserve peace and harmony no private piques or quarrels must be brought within the door of the Lodge, far less any quarrel about Religions or National or State-Policy, we being only, as Masons, of the religion in which all men agree; and we are also of all Nations, Tongues, Kindreds and Languages, and are resolved against all Politics as what never yet conduced to the welfare of the Lodge, nor ever will.

Such is the principle on which Masonry rests, and the spirit in which it has toiled through the ages, breaking down barriers of caste and creed, of race and rank, creating reverence, not only for the Divine, but also for the Human — for man as man, regardless of land or language, for the right of every man to be free of body and soul and have a place in the sun — and drawing men together in mutual respect into a profound and far-reaching fellowship. Never was its benign spirit more needed than today, living, as we are, in a world of fratricidal strife, when every energy of the race seems dedicated to destruction.

Alas, that the truth of the Brotherhood of Man should be revealed only in tragedy and terror, but if the sword of Mars stabs the world wide awake to this fact, by the very magnitude of the horror of war, it will be worth the price in suffering. Truly, the time has come when Masonry must take up its harp and strike its world-chord with all its might— strike it magnificently and with prophetic stroke.

Human unity is no fanciful dream of a poet, no far off promise of a prophet; it is a fact. Geographical boundaries do not now and never have represented either race or national potencies. Morality, intelligence, efficiency, fraternity refuse racial or political labels. There is no German chemistry, no British astronomy, no Russian mathematics. What is most excellent in Russia—its Tolstoys, its Kropotkins, its musicians, its painters, and its hard-handed millions of toilers—is not Russian, but human. The same is true of Germany, France and England. Goethe and Schiller, Koch and Kant are fellow-countrymen of Shakespeare and Darwin, of Hugo and Pasteur. The Republic of Letters and of Science is universal; it is only our patriotism that has lagged behind and become "the virtue of narrow minds" —when, indeed, it is not actually what Johnson called it, "the last resort of knaves."

How, then, can we justify our love of our own land as over against those who hold that all patriotism is provincial, if not pernicious? Only in this way: Each nation, each race has a genius of its own, and by that fact a contribution to make and a service to render to the total of humanity. Judea was no larger than Iowa, and yet it gave to the race its loftiest and truest religion, and the strongest, whitest, sweetest soul the earth has known. Greece was a tiny land, girt about by violet seas, but it added immeasurable wealth of art, drama and philosophy to the world. So of Rome. And thus we might call the roll of races and nations, asking of each what it had or has to give of beauty and of truth to mankind. Even so, our country has a genius unique, particular, and peculiar, and by that token a service to render to the universal life of humanity. What is that service if it be not to show, not only that "government of the People, by the People, for the People shall not perish from the earth," but that it is the highest ideal of government, and that it makes for the greatest happiness of man, alike in private nobility and public welfare? Of that genius and service our flag is the emblem and prophecy, and loyalty to that emblem implies devotion to that service. Our field is the world, but our solicitude is our own country—that it may the better make its unique and priceless contribution to the universal good. Thus, with due reverence for other nations, by loyalty to our own flag we best serve our race.

Above all nations, greater than all races, more important than all royalties is Humanity, and no one nation can live to itself, much less be truly great, without regard for the usefulness and happiness of other nations. What we need is a transvaluation of patriotism from a tribal loyalty into a universal allegiance—a world-patriotism, growing out of the deepening sense of human solidarity, large of outlook, far-reaching and benign of spirit. As it is now, patriotism consists too much in loving our own land and hating every other — a feeling unworthy of a Republic where Teuton, Saxon, Slav, Gaul, Celt live amicably together, stand shoulder to shoulder in the industrial army, eat out of the same dinner pails, and, to a surprising degree, worship at the same altar.

V

Exactly; and that is the very genius of Freemasonry, its mission to mankind, and the spirit which it seeks to make prevail. By its very nature cosmopolitan, it thinks in terms of Humanity, rather than of race or creed or party, being as the old German Handbook defined it, the activity of closely united men who, employing symbolical forms borrowed from architecture work for the welfare of humanity, striving morally to ennoble themselves and others, and thereby to bring about "a universal league of mankind, which they aspire to exhibit, even now, on a small scale." As Goethe said, in his poem on "The Lodge,"

The Mason's ways are
A type of existence,
And his persistence
Is, as the days are
Of men in this world.

Every Lodge is an emblem and prophecy of the world, and there will be no abiding peace on earth until what Masonry exhibits on a small scale is made worldwide, and its spirit of goodwill among men of all ranks, races and religions becomes the reigning genius of humanity. Other way out of war there is none. If, instead of meeting behind closed doors for intrigue, the men who plotted this war had met in a Masonic Lodge, not one of them would have drawn a sword! Alas, Lilliputian militarists have kindled a fire which not even Gulliver can put out, spreading death and desolation every whither — fanning old feuds, marshalling hordes of hates, until the very existence of civilization is threatened.

What of the future? One thing is evident: if this tragedy drags its bloody way to the bitter end, as now seems likely, every tie by which man is bound to man the world over will be needed to hold the race together; and Masonry is one of those ties. To that end, Masonry itself must recapture its old accent and emphasis upon universal principles, and take part in recruiting and mobilizing a great army of men of goodwill, if so we may dehorn the nations now goring each other to death, and bring to this passion-clouded earth the light of reason. War is waste. It is unreason. It settles nothing. It is devolution, not evolution. It is not the survival of the fittest, but the sacrifice of the best. The canker of long peace, as Shakespeare called it, is the canker not of peace, but of materialism. No;

The crest and crowning of all good,
Life's final star, is Brotherhood;
For it will bring again to Earth
Her long-lost Poesy and Mirth;
Will send new light on every face,
A kingly power upon the race.
And till it comes we men are slaves,
And travel downward to the dust of graves.

What this sad world needs is a League of its "Large Eternal Fellows," tall enough of soul to look over barriers of race, walls of creed, and mountains of misunderstanding, and recognize their kinsmen in every land and language. These are the men who see that we are in more danger from the grasping greed and blind ambition of the few who rule than we ever were, ever will or ever can be from the great, toiling masses of our fellows in other lands. They see that the great generalship displayed in the war, and its good comradeship — the sagacity of its leaders, and the singing, jesting courage with which the youth of Europe is marching to the grave — are the very qualities which, if dedicated to the organization of the world upon a basis of peace, will swing the earth into a new orbit! Therefore.

Come, clear the way, then, clear the way:
Blind creeds and kings have had their day.
Break the dead branches from the path:
Our hope is in the aftermath —
Our hope is in heroic men,
Star-led to build the world again,
To this event the ages ran:
Make way for Brotherhood — make way for Man !